Family Therapy:

Exploring the field's past, present and possible futures

Edited by

David Denborough

DULWICH CENTRE PUBLICATIONS
Adelaide, South Australia

ISBN 978-0-9577929-4-4

Copyright © 2001 by
Dulwich Centre Publications
Hutt St PO Box 7192
Adelaide 5000, South Australia
phone (61-8) 8223 3966, fax (61-8) 8232 4441
email: dcp@senet.com.au
website: www.dulwichcentre.com.au

Contents

Bringing it Back Home to Australia

Introduction

by

David Denborough

As I hold the manuscript of this book in my hand I am reminded of all the conversations that are recorded within it. These conversations have taken place in people's homes, in rooms of conference venues, in the foyers of hotels, and in various cafés in Australia, New Zealand, Norway, the USA and the UK. For short periods of time, influential practitioners have invited me, and now you the reader, into their worldview and the history that has shaped it. In some circumstances they have offered reflections and regrets about aspects of past practices, and they have spoken of what continues to inspire them.

It is my hope that for those of my generation, for whom the origins of family therapy took place well before our birth, this book can act as an introduction to the people and events that have led us to the present day. I hope that this book enables you to not only engage with the diversity of ideas of the field but also to get to know, in some small way, those whose stories are contained in these pages.

I particularly hope that you find this a friendly and accessible book, for these are the words I would use to describe the interviews that are recorded here.

It can be difficult to convey on paper the warmth of someone's smile, the twinkle of their eye, or the kindness that has characterised a conversation. So let me just say here, that every interview contained in this book was offered in a spirit of kindness, thoughtfulness and generosity.

The degree of openness shown by those who were interviewed has seemed especially significant, as has the respect demonstrated to each other. Those interviewed represent significantly different philosophies and practices to one another, and most feel that it is important that these differences be articulated and understood. And yet, in every conversation, it was the ideas that were being discussed and engaged with. Time and again it was made clear that despite the significant differences, all those interviewed are in some way linked to each other through the history of the field and respect for each other's contributions.

The field of family therapy, like everything else, has been significantly shaped by its times. When the field first began, in North America in the late 1950s, the ideas of what constituted a family were very different than they are today. The second wave of feminism, gay liberation, sexual liberation, changing attitudes to children, and social movements aimed at addressing indigenous rights, racism and other issues of culture, continue to significantly shape and re-shape the field of family therapy as they do all aspects of life.

The field of family therapy is constantly changing and now is no exception. For therapists of my generation, the current changes represent ongoing creativity and excitement. And yet, as we continue to explore new directions, it will be imperative that we have our history close by. I hope that this book contributes in some small way to ensuring that this is possible.

There are many further interviews that ideally would have been included here, and perhaps somewhere down the track compiling these will be possible. But for now, I hope you enjoy the following interviews which I had the pleasure of editing. I think you'll agree that they make intriguing reading.

Acknowledgements

Although I conducted and edited the interviews that are contained here, this publication was a collaborative endeavour. The idea for this book came from Cheryl White and Dulwich Centre Publications provided the resources and support to make it possible. The reason why I was welcomed by so many people wherever I went was due to long histories of friendship and professional relationship that were generously opened up by Cheryl White and Michael White. I'd also like to acknowledge the editorial assistance of Sky Laris, and the layout work of Jane Hales.

There are two further acknowledgements that I feel are important to make. Firstly, to all those interviewed for this book - not only for their generosity in relation to these particular conversations, but also for the years that they have dedicated to trying to find ways of working with families that will make a difference. And finally, a more general acknowledgement - to all those practitioners for whom this book has been written. I work as I writer, one step back from those of you who are working with individuals and families every day. I admire the work that you do and I hope this book provides you sustenance and some sense of company.

About the interviews in this book

A number of these interviews took place at the Family Therapy World Congress in Oslo, Norway, from 14th-17th June 2000. Further interviews took place in Boston, New York City, London, Oxford, Auckland and Adelaide over the course of 2000-2001. To bring the discussions back to an Australian context, two interviews took place at the Australian & New Zealand Family Therapy Conference held in Canberra from 4th-7th July 2000.

1

Looking towards solutions

an interview with

Insoo Kim Berg

Insoo Kim Berg is one of the originators, with Steve de Shazer, of the widely popular and highly respected Solution-Focused Therapy. The following interview took place in Oslo, Norway, at the Family Therapy World Congress where Insoo was giving a plenary on 'Reconciliation in clinical work'.

Insoo, what was the context in which you and others began to develop what has come to be known as Solution-Focused Family Therapy?

Like most people of my generation, I was trained in a psycho-dynamic approach. I was a very good student, memorised everything I was taught and tried to put it into practice. A couple of important things happened. In the late 1960s and early 1970s America was struggling with the Vietnam war and veterans from this war were returning. Increasing numbers of these young men came back with severe drug and alcohol problems and what we would now call flashbacks – but this word was not invented then. In fact, post-traumatic stress disorder was not formally described until around 1982. It was ten years before we had a language to describe the effects of people's experiences of extreme trauma.

There was a particular incident in Milwaukee that I recall. One of the young men who came back from Vietnam always had nightmares in which he was being chased by Vietcong soldiers. He was so scared that he slept with a gun under his pillow. In the middle of one night, however, he woke from his nightmares and shot and killed his wife – thinking that she was a member of the Vietcong coming to attack him. This event made newspaper headlines at a time when the generations were polarised about the Vietnam war.

The veterans coming back were very young people, mostly twenty or twenty-one who had been drafted, served a year, and had had terrible experiences. They were very disillusioned and even when they needed help, many would not go to veterans' hospitals because they did not trust the army anymore.

I had an intimate understanding of the horrors of war because from 1950-53, as a young teenager in Korea I was a refugee from my home and wandered the countryside until the war ended. I came to the US as a student and I had finished my education and was working as a young therapist when this episode with a veteran happened. I looked around and realised that most Americans had no experience of being in the middle of a war like these young returning veterans had been, and I had been. I knew what it felt like to be shot at, bombed at, to go hungry and to be scared all the time for your life.

I thought I would offer whatever little experience I had so I started a group for these young men. I was very naïve, with a good heart, not knowing quite what to do. I sought out the best help I could find. I managed to find a very competent, psychoanalytically orientated consultant in the community who would meet with me. I would tell the stories of the young men and sometimes I was so desperate for assistance that I would videotape the sessions and take the tapes to the consultant. I also decided I needed more training and began to commute to a training program at Menninger Clinic in Kansas. I would take my tapes and ask supervisors, 'Please tell me what to do, how can I help these people?'

At around this time, one of the supervisors turned to me and said, 'Well what is your counter-transference issue with this group of young men?' I said, 'What do you mean?' I didn't know what he was talking about. And he said, 'Well, you know, these are the soldiers who killed your people'. I still didn't know what he was talking about! I come from Korea and their war was in Vietnam – thousands of miles away. The supervisor didn't understand this. He thought that everybody 'over there' was all the same. I was absolutely shocked at first and then profoundly devastated. What he was implying was that I was affected by what is known as the 'Stockholm syndrome' – where prisoners identify with the people who imprison them and immediately take their side. That was the beginning of me ending my association with psychoanalytic theory and therapy.

In my work with these young men, I realised something that I never read anywhere, that nobody ever told me about. It was very painful to sit and listen to these young men week after week talking about how they had killed women and children, and about how their buddies were killed and injured in front of them. Even now, thinking about these stories brings great sadness to me.

These young men were supposedly 'dysfunctional people' because there were other soldiers returning who did not have the kind of problems that they were experiencing. The commonly held explanation was that these young men must have been dysfunctional *before* they went to war, that these young men were pre-disposed in some way to the reactions they were now displaying. Various words were used to describe these young men. They were seen to be 'disintegrating' or 'vertically splitting'.

But despite the fact that these young men were supposed to be very dysfunctional people, they were going to university and taking various classes. They would come to the meetings with a book bag on their backs, on their way to class or on the way back. Many of them held jobs. Many had girlfriends. They were able to establish relationships with some people. The contradiction puzzled me. How can they do these things? If they are so dysfunctional, how can they still be functioning enough to do these things?

I was also confused because they were telling me such terrible stories. Some of the things they had done were terrible and yet they were very nice, thoughtful, polite, and kind young men. I was so surprised, so shocked. They seemed to me very nice people. I started to see some cracks between what I had learned, what I was taught, and what I was observing. And I think this was the beginning of my search for something other than what I was taught. This was in the early 1970s.

Other writers in the field of family therapy were challenging conventional ways of understanding therapy and families. Jay Haley's book, 'Strategies of Psychotherapy' (which had come out in 1963) influenced a lot of people of my generation. It was the first book that opened up to me in a clearly explained way an alternative way of looking at things. It showed me that there are different ways of looking at the same event. It challenged me to find my own way of looking at what was happening and to come up with my own way of working.

Can you say a little about some of the alternative ways of working that you, along with others, then began to develop?

The psychoanalytic approach had been one way of explaining change, while the theory of change of the Mental Research Institute (MRI) made more sense to me. It was a way of explaining change that embraced differences. I was raised as a Christian in a very Buddhist culture. I knew my family was very different from other families and that there was nothing unusual about being different. Being Asian in America from 1957 onwards also meant that difference was something with which I was familiar. Difference, to me, was just a part of life.

So this in some way also contributed to moving away from any pathological understanding of difference?

Yes. Most Westerners seem to think of culture as some kind of object that can be acquired, given or taken away. But culture is so much a part of you, I don't think we even realise the ways it affects our thinking and breathing. Living in America, I had to be more aware of who I was because I was constantly reminded of my differences and became more aware of what is cultural. It has been a wonderful experience in that way. It has offered a sense of who I am, what I am, how I am different and how I am similar.

So how do you think that those experiences and different knowledges of life contributed to the work that you are doing? How did that translate into practice?

The notion of focusing on pathology did not make sense to me. Where do you draw the line between what is normal and what is abnormal? The question is absurd. In some ways I grew up very differently from my neighbours, my colleagues, but in other ways my childhood was very similar. How can we judge a childhood or a family in terms of normality? So we moved right away from these ways of thinking.

So, in stepping aside from those judgements of normality or abnormality, of functional or dysfunctional families, can you say a little bit about how the emphasis of the work also shifted to looking at solutions rather than at problems?

When Steve de Shazer, myself and others established the Brief Family Therapy Center in Milwaukee in the mid 1970s our initial dream was that we would establish a Midwest version of MRI. But just as I'd started to see a little crack in psychoanalytic theory, we also noticed that there were lots of times when the people who came to consult with us weren't affected by problems. At the time the language of the MRI and others was describing 'problem-maintenance patterns', or the 'attempted solution is the problem'. The primary intervention involved disrupting attempted solutions because, out of this, would come real change. Gradually this kind of notion stopped making a lot of sense to us.

    The changes to our thinking came out of the clinical work itself. I was initially trained as a pharmacist. With this natural science training came a belief that observation is a very important part of the training. If what you observe and what you believe do not match then you need to question either what you are observing or what you believe. Once we started observing what was working in the lives of the families we were seeing, we stopped focusing on the problems in people's lives and instead moved the focus to their solutions, that is, what worked for them.

We began to focus on what people were still doing well, how they were doing this and how this know-how could apply to solutions in other aspects of their lives so their lives would be more satisfying to them. Rather than looking for and then addressing pathologies, we began to encourage families to recognise their competencies. We became increasingly interested in the family's competencies as these can be built upon. We felt we needed to recognise what was working in families and not to interfere with this. If it ain't broke, don't fix it.

We also began to believe that it was important for the family to set goals for the therapy which we as therapists could then work towards. Once these goals had been set we could then enquire about times when the family members were able to have a little peace of mind, or hang onto their job, etc. We began to focus on exceptions, even when they seemed insignificant. By exploring these times and what was different about themselves, clients can find solutions to their current difficulties.

This new orientation brought various developments including 'the miracle question': 'Suppose one night, while you were asleep, there was a miracle and this problem was solved. How would you know? What would be different?' Not only does this question help to set goals but it enables conversations to begin to happen about solutions.

Are there any other defining aspects of this early work that would be good to mention?

We had a very interesting team. Steve and I are sort of the spokespeople for the team, but we had a collection of very unusual and talented people from all kinds of backgrounds. Steve's background was as a musician and painter, my background was as a pharmacist. We also had a linguist, a sociologist, and an educator. This variety was deliberate as it really helped us to look at things from multiple perspectives. It also often led to heated debate! Trainees also helped enormously with their questions.

The ways of working that your team originated have been enormously influential and have been taken up in a wide range of places. Would you like to talk about this?

Actually, there are a lot of things that we are worried about in relation to how people take and apply what we are discussing. Just yesterday I heard someone describing our work as an orthodoxy, as a very rigid form of therapy. They were saying that in order to do brief therapy you have to do this, and then this, and then this. I didn't know what to say.

Like any model we have tried to describe what we do, but the process of description and the ways in which people read these descriptions can be very different than what actually happens. I have always had to pay attention to the English language because I had to learn it when I came to the US in 1957. It is not my mother tongue. We have done our best to try to describe our ways of working, to provide some outlines for people to think about. To hear that people think that we are saying that this is the only way to do it, that it is a rigid form of therapy, is surprising. Perhaps it is due to the inadequacy of language to describe a therapy session. Therapeutic conversation is such a complex activity and cannot be reduced to simple steps. When people seem to think that Insoo says you have to do this first, and then that second, I feel like saying, 'Give me a break!' It's amazing that ten years later something you have written can come back to haunt you.

What is your sense about the family therapy field generally? What are some of the issues that you think people are trying to grapple with?

It has been very heartening to step outside of the US and attend this conference. Family therapy started as rebellion against certain things. Now it appears we have become our own establishment and rebellion is no longer necessary. It seems to me that in the US we are floundering around saying what do we rebel against next? We used to be so certain what we were against, but now we are not so certain. Once we had powerful Freud that we had to fight against but this is no longer true. Freudian thinking is really losing its grip. I am not sure where the next surge of energy is going to come from. I feel like the field has lost some energy so it is really reassuring to see at this conference that in places outside western culture, work with families is vibrant and alive. There is also a real diversity of thought here and that is lovely to see.

What are some of the areas of work which you are currently interested in?

Over the last five years I have been spending a lot of time with organisations that respond to child abuse and neglect. Over the last thirty years US society decided that we were not going to accept child abuse and this of course has been a very good thing. But we haven't really known how to go about addressing the complexities of this issue. We didn't know how to respond to parents who end up abusing or neglecting their children. We saw them narrowly as perpetrators rather than placing their lives in context and trying to respond to their experience in some effective way. In my opinion, we have treated these parents very badly. I have been working in one state to try to reform the ways in which services are provided to families. System change does not just happen by working with the people at the lower level. We have to work up and down the entire hierarchy, and this is happening. After five years we are now seeing some small changes. There are hopeful signs.

We are paying attention to what is working in those systems and building upon them. We are interviewing social workers whose dedication and creative ideas powerfully challenge the commonplace depiction of social workers as untrained, overworked and uninformed. It is social workers who have to interview families and try to establish whether abuse is taking place. We are now thinking of these interviews not only as interventions but also as preventive work. We believe that the one interview can serve as an investigation, prevention and treatment. Looking at these issues simultaneously is offering us a lot of hope for change. We want social workers to train other social workers in how this can take place.

There is much work to be done, but I honestly believe that these systems can be turned around. The impossible does sometimes occur. The theme of this conference is Reconciliation: Voices for a new era. At this precise moment in Korea events of reconciliation are taking place that are completely beyond what I would have ever imagined would take place in my lifetime. As long as we keep looking towards solutions, I will never doubt what can be overcome.

2

The inevitable journey from individual to family therapy

an interview with

Salvador Minuchin

Salvador Minuchin is considered one of the founders of the field of family therapy. As the originator of Structural Family Therapy, his influence on the field has been profound. This interview took place in the home of Salvador Minuchin and Patricia Minuchin in Boston, USA in September 2000. Salvador Minuchin, Cheryl White and David Denborough were present. David Denborough was the interviewer.

Last night, as you were showing us around this apartment, I was drawn to the photograph of you that was taken in Palestine / Israel in 1948. I was wondering if to start this interview you'd be interested in speaking about how you came to be in that part of the world at that time and how you moved from there to your work with 'Families in the Slums'

I am presently writing a book of memoirs with the title of 'the inevitable journey from individual to family therapy'. I call this an inevitable journey because it was inevitable for me. Clearly it is not inevitable more generally as many people remain involved in individual therapy. But for me, to move from individual therapy to family therapy was inevitable based on my history and its trajectory.

I am a Jew who was born in Argentina in a small town. I grew up as the 'other'. Whereas in Australia 'the other' are Aboriginal Australians, and here in North America the 'other' are often African Americans, in Argentina, I was the other, Jews were the other. This experience of growing up being discriminated against creates, in my opinion, particular psychological determinants.

From the day I was born, my ethnicity as a Jew, my Jewishness has influenced how others have defined my identity and how I have defined myself. For instance, as Jews, we live an interesting dichotomy or paradox. We need to be invisible and we need to prove ourselves, resist our discrimination, by being better than the other. My father would say to me as I was growing up, 'If you succeed they should not see you, but you need to succeed.' I grew up as a competitor, needing to be better than the others. I also grew up as a fighter – a physical fighter – and I believe this too had a cultural component. The concept of fighting as a minority is an interesting one. If you are a member of a minority group then your aggression in many ways is seen as permissible. It is not seen as aggression but instead liberation. Trying to pass as non-Jewish, trying as a Jewish person to compete and to surpass the achievements of others, and fighting for a place to establish a place in the world, were all ways in which Jewishness defined me as a person.

And so in 1948 I went to Israel to participate in the Israeli war of liberation. Certainly it was not a war of liberation for the Arabs but it was the war of Israeli liberation and I was determined to be a part of it. It was only a few years since the world had learned of the truth of the Holocaust and we knew that it was necessary for the survival of Jewish people to establish a Jewish state. I was there in 1948-49 during the war and I then came back to the United States, to become a psychiatrist.

I believe that after you trained here in the US you returned to Israel to work for a period of time. Is that correct?

Yes. After training in child psychiatry I returned to Israel where I worked in an organisation that was bringing children, who were without their families, to Israel. The Hebrew word for immigration to Israel is aliya – which has the implication of ascending. The organisation was bringing to Israel children who were survivors of the Holocaust, and then later children from other parts of the world, mostly from Africa. I was therefore working with children from multiple ethnicities and who looked very different from one another. I recall a time when I was working with a Chinese-Jewish child, a Danish-Jewish child and a Yemenite Jewish child.

Although I was working only with Jewish people, there was a tremendous historical and cultural diversity. Over centuries, Jewish people have engaged with and taken on the cultural characteristics of the people wherever they have lived. There has also been a tremendous amount of genetic interchange, some of which occurred through pogroms and rapes, but also through choice. As I was working with these multiple ethnic groups, I found the question of ethnic diversity and context intriguing.

Gradually though, I came to see that the concept of the individual child, which I had been trained in, and the concept of ethnic diversity were in conflict. Within child psychiatry there was no platform for uniting these two elements. I was an individual child psychiatrist trained psycho-dynamically and I was a cultural anthropologist observing culture. In one I was a professional and in the other I was an amateur observer, but I could find no way to bring these two entities together. In hindsight, this was one of the experiences early in my professional career that evoked questions about individuals and how the broader context of their lives need to be considered within therapy.

When I returned to the US, I trained as an analyst and then began working at an institution for delinquent children. Here, I found myself caught between the internalised life of the boys and the life of the black ghetto. The centre of the therapeutic world at this time was seen to be the internalised life of child. The social life of the child played no part within the clinical approach. There were some sociologists who wrote about the rules that informed the behaviours of adolescent children living in gangs, but their inquiries and those of the child psychiatrists would never meet. As child psychiatrists of the time, we were concerned only with the internal story of the individual, the broader context of people's lives needed to disappear.

I imagine then, that it was from this place that you and others began the journey that led to the creation of the field of family therapy ...

Yes. The inevitable journey began to try to resolve the complexity of trying to answer the question – how do we in therapy attend to the broader context of people's lives? Individual psycho-dynamic psychiatry of the time stipulated that the broader context of someone's life has always been internalised and therefore it was possible to dismiss the current context of someone's life as mere disturbance. But it became apparent that the current context of people's lives was operating at the same time in influential ways. How to reconcile these two elements was the inevitable journey that led to the creation of family therapy.

In my view, family therapy grew from the beginning in a dichotomous manner. The two main intellectual leaders of early family therapy were Nathan Ackerman and Gregory Bateson.

Ackerman was a clinician, a child psychiatrist and an analyst. Bateson was an anthropologist and a thinker.

Ackerman was a very significant clinician and wrote some of the first family therapy books. He continued in many ways to be an analyst but the analysis became focused on the construction of how family systems operated through the interdigitation of individuals' psyches.

Bateson, on the other hand, was not a clinician, he was a man of concepts. He brought to the field ideas that are tremendously important – ecology, systems, cybernetics, and a concern that psychologists ought not to touch. He brought to the field the idea that if you enter into a culture you need to be very concerned about your influence upon it.

In these early years, following the differing directions of Ackerman and Bateson, two different traditions were established within the family therapy field – traditions that influence practice to this day. In one grouping, or tradition, are those I would refer to as the intervening therapists. I would include myself in this grouping. These clinicians were all psychoanalysts by training, or psycho-dynamically orientated. We had all undergone psychoanalysis ourselves and believed in the importance of the unconscious. But we had come to oppose the static position of the therapist in psychoanalysis. In the 1950s, various neo Freudian cultural therapists, including Erich Fromm, Erik Erickson, Abraham Kardiner, Karen Honey and Harry Stack Sullivan had begun to question how psychoanalysis focussed solely on intra-psychic processes. Harry Stack Sullivan, the creator of the interpersonal school of psychoanalysis, said that psychoanalysis was a process between two people, the psychoanalyst and the patient. Rather than seeing counter-transference reactions as something negative, the neo Freudians saw it as sources of genuine understanding. Building on this awareness that the therapist is a part of the system, Ackerman, and a number of others, wanted to step in more actively and intervene. We had come to believe that the therapists' job was to induce change. In the same group as Ackerman were Whitaker, Nagy, Bowen, Satir, Haley and myself. We were all people who felt comfortable with the idea, in fact who were certain that it was our role, to enter into a field of family relations and produce change.

From Bateson came the contrary idea. As an anthropologist he was interested in what makes cultures change and was cautious of interventions in a culture. As an anthropologist he was wary of the disturbing influence of the therapists' point of view on the culture of the family.

Following the tradition initiated by Bateson came the work of the Mental Research Institute which was focused on the question, 'How can family therapists intervene minimally in the families they meet with? How can the potential damage done by family therapists be controlled and minimised?' This is not an easy question and it still concerns those who are influenced by the Bateson tradition – Brief therapists, Solution Focused therapists, the Milan School, and those influenced by ideas of social constructionism.

Over the years, different methods have been developed by those determined to reduce the potential harm of therapy. The Milan group replaced the therapist with the team, and instead of interpretations, questions were used as the basis of therapy. In Brief therapy, the therapist asks the patients what do they want to address and then works towards this outcome in ten sessions. Many other methods have also been developed including the use of reflecting teams and externalising conversations.

Although I can see that some of these methods are respectful and democratic, and very good techniques, the therapists in these schools approach the work from a completely different theory of change than I do. For those of us who believe it is our responsibility as therapists to enter into a field of family relations and induce change, the idea of embracing 'not-knowing' for example, is quite absurd. All clinicians know that therapists do exert influence, that therapists are not objective and neutral, and that they are in a hierarchical position towards the family. But different therapists have different theories of change and this is what is important to me. These differences have existed from the beginning of the field. Broadly speaking, there have been those of us who believe in our responsibilities to make interventions, and those who try to find ways of facilitating change but are careful of distorting the field in which they intervene. To my mind, this can all be traced back to Ackerman and Bateson.

Can you tell me more about what those early days of the family therapy field were like. I have the sense that they were exciting times…

The first article about the family that was influential in the field of therapy was by Jackson in 1957. He wrote about families even though he was still an individual analyst. I started working with families after Jackson's article in 1958-59. And around this time the field of family therapy then developed like an eruption in the mental health field. This was a period of great workshops with audiences of 300, 400, 500 people in which therapists such as Bowen, Satir, Haley, Whitaker and myself would interact a little like jazz musicians. We would carry our video tapes with us wherever we would go and the conversations that were being shared were full of energy. This was a time when family therapy took a kind of populist bent because for the first time therapists would actually present their work to others. We would show videos in workshops. What you see today as natural is absolutely new. It was a dramatic break from past practices and many people were against it. It would be unheard of for a video of a psychoanalysis session to be shared with others. People were very concerned about issues of privacy. But we were a part of something new and we realised that bringing therapy out of private therapy rooms so it could be discussed and critiqued was going to be crucial.

There was a great deal of competition and collaboration in those days. We were all friends. I recall going with Lyman Wynn to observe Whitaker work for a week. We were all so keen to learn from one another. With Virginia Satir, I had for decades a competitive kind of bantering. It was a relationship that was competitive and generative. Virginia was the goddess of family therapy. Whenever she gave workshops it always seemed as if there were thousands of people. There is a story I have heard that could possibly be true, that she once held a workshop in a football field!

Anything seemed possible in the 1960s and early 70s. It was a golden period when family therapy blossomed. Early on, the MRI was the centre of this energy. But in the later 60s to mid 70s the Philadelphia Child Guidance Centre became the centre of the field. Whitaker's work was also very important – it is a shame that you can not interview him. He was a great person and not recognised enough for his contributions. Bowen's contributions were also important. His work went on to influence significant therapists such as Betty Carter and Monica McGoldrick. In the late 1960s the Milano Team became the first non-American group to significantly influence the field.

In time, we began to explore our own areas. My therapy was different from that of others because I began to work with different populations. I was working with families from the slums, with African American and Hispanic young people and their families. On working with these families I had to try to develop ways of speaking and working that would be fit in this context. It was a continual challenge and this was very generative.

These were exciting times, but during this excitement, one thing that happened to the field was that we abandoned the individual. As we talked about systems we dismissed the individual. This was a great loss. There were articles in the beginning of the field that plainly stated that family therapy could only be done if all the family members were present.

Now, I have the opposite worry. I am concerned that the family is being lost in the field of family therapy. This also has a history. As those at the MRI began to follow Bateson's inquiry as to how to limit therapists' interventions they found that sometimes they could influence the behaviour of the child by working only with the parents, or by working with the individual. With this, in my mind comes the beginning of the dismissal of the family. Some of the current approaches influenced by Bateson, and more recently social constructionism, are losing the emphasis that the field of family therapy strived so hard to create – that being to consider the lives of individuals within the context of their family relationships and to develop ways of working with all these relationships.

To fully explain what I think is at risk if we were to lose the family from family therapy I need to define family therapy. I would say that family therapy is an intervention to help people to help each other in their significant systems. It is the only therapeutic intervention in which what you want is to help husbands to help wives, wives to help husbands, parents to help children, children to help parents. It is a very generous and humanistic kind of intervention in which you are trying to say to people there is a way in which you can be competent and assist those around you to live differently to the ways they have been living. In this way family therapy is about creating a language to utilise the healing capacity of family members. To me that is what family therapy is, and I think it is fantastic notion! It saddens me that in the US, we have not realised the potential that we dreamed in the 1970s.

That is a sadness that some others that I have interviewed have also spoken about. Can you say a little more about this?

In the 1970s I was certain that family therapy would be thriving by now. There is no doubt that we have made significant inroads, especially in relation to working with poor people. We will continue to be able to influence the organisations that work with poor communities to think of families instead of individuals because it is a more economic and efficient way of working. But the middle classes are still overwhelmingly using individual therapy and psychiatry. I don't underestimate the influence of the powerful coalition between the pharmaceutical industry and psychiatry. In many ways the energy that was once associated with family therapy is now associated with organic psychiatry. In some ways economic imperatives are competing with what family therapy proposes – that a complex response is required to address complex situations. As family therapists, I believe that we need to think how can we successfully convey our ideas in a climate so driven by economics.

What about within the field of family therapy? I know that you have been having various conversations about current directions of the field and some concerns you have in relation to narrative ideas and post-structuralist thinking...

As I mentioned earlier I am concerned about the dismissal of the family from some approaches to family therapy. I am also concerned about the postmodern dismissal of universals. Just as in the beginning of family therapy one of the problems we faced in talking about systems was how we missed the individual, now one of the hazards that I see in the narrative approach is that in trying to deal with diversity, there is the potential to miss the universals. I have concerns about the ways in which narrative therapists and others are engaging with postmodern ideas. I think that the postmodernists have a most interesting theoretical conundrum. As I understand it, postmodernists set themselves up as anti-universals. Universals are dismissed but what you have is a universal decree. I have been involved in a dialogue with the field about this. There are however, aspects of the politics of the postmodernists that I am drawn to. As a Marxist in my earlier years, we were very interested in the ways in which the dominant culture was controlling representations in the media and so forth. I find many of the concepts of Foucault in relation to this tremendously interesting.

In fact, to me, the biggest problem in family therapy at this point is the lack of diversity. In the early days there was a competitive diversity, and an expanding diversity. These days this is not true and this is a big loss. I believe that there needs to be more dialogue across points of difference.

It has certainly been a great experience for me to speak with family therapists from a wide range of perspectives. One of the unexpected things that have come from the conversations has been to hear of the diversity of influences and experiences that people have brought to the field of family therapy. I'd like to ask you a little about this. I know that apart from your clinical work, your writing and your teaching, you have also been engaged with the theatre. And the ways in which you use the written word has been very significant to so many people. I'd love to ask you about how you see the links between therapy, the written word, enactment, drama and theatre...and how these links have played out in your work and life...

When I was younger I always wanted to be a writer. I wrote poetry for a number of years and I have gained a great sense of pleasure in having written two plays – one of which was produced, if only for an audience of family therapists and only for two evenings, and I worked with the actors and the director. This was a great honour and I just loved it! I later saw the same play in Holland, in Dutch, again for a family therapy audience and also for two evenings, and I saw the difference that a director can do with a play. In the US the director was a woman and the play became feminist and the main character became a heroine. In Holland the director who was a man, highlighted a different character whose view of life was sardonic.

When I think about the use of language in my life I am brought back to the fact that I am a foreigner to this country and foreigners develop a view of language that is different. Samuel Beckett knew this very well. So well that he chose to write in French, even though he was Irish. It is extraordinary that he chose to write in French but he felt that in a foreign language he could make his words more precise. He was tremendously concerned with the sparcity of language.

I grew up speaking a poetic Spanish and then developed an inarticulate English. I was also working with a population here in the US that spoke American Slang. I really entered into worlds in which I was in some ways 'apart from' language. From this sense of being a foreigner both to this country but also to the subcultures in which I was working, I developed a metaphoric language. Sometimes I think was due to a lack of precision, but it was also the therapeutic style that I crafted. When I do therapy, I continuously talk metaphorically and the metaphors I evoke work in many directions at once.

All therapists use language differently. Michael White's use of language in therapy, in relation to his scaffolding of questions, for example, is very precise. I admire this, especially as I was raised within Talmudic traditions of scholarship which highly value such precision. However, my language in therapy is different, it is a language of metaphor.

In my interventions I took a great interest in enactment. Rather than simply talking about or describing situations and problems that occur at home or elsewhere outside of the therapy room, we would invite families to display the patterns there and then. We were very interested in the ways in which people acted out events and situations in the therapy room. Through enactment, the therapist has the chance to witness behaviours and the emotions associated with them. The therapist sees people sweat and move, and therapy takes place not only in the realm of language but experience.

My engagement with enactment derived directly from my theatrical interest and a belief that the staging of events organises meaning. In all these ways, I believe that my relationship to language and to theatre has been linked to my therapy.

One of the ways in which I came to be engaged with family therapy was that while I was working in prisons, and also in schools with young men in relation to issues of gender and violence, I came across a Dulwich Centre Newsletter focusing on issues of gender, masculinity and working with men. You were talking earlier about how different your play looked in the theatre when directed by a feminist woman and when directed by a man, I'd love to hear your views on how family therapy has tried to grapple with those issues of gender...

That is an area to which I came very late. My interest from the beginning was focused on issues of poverty and issues of class. From a socialist perspective, issues of class were clear to me. Ethnicity came later. Initially I did not see class and ethnicity together. I responded to class and then as an after thought I saw the ways in which ethnicity and class were inter-related.

Gender I did not see. I come from a Spanish culture, and next month I will be 79 – older than your father, I imagine! I grew up in a completely different world. The first time I saw gender as a social phenomenom was when the University of Pennsylvania reimbursed Pat Minuchin, my wife, who was a professor, because her salary had been lower than that of her male counterparts. Only then did I start to see gender as a political and economic issue.

To understand gender as political was a new direction for me. I always saw male and female roles as a complementarity. I come from a family in which my parents never divorced. They were married until they died and they had a traditional organisation of the family. My father did certain things, my mother did others and I saw that as harmonious. What's more, later this year I will have been married for fifty years, and I would say that my relationship with Pat is harmoniously complementary. Where issues of power exist, they exist in dialogue. The idea of disparity, of lack of balance between men and women was not part of my perception of the world.

When the feminist challenge came to family therapy I recall Marion Walters pointing out the sexist ways in which I had organised the Philadelphia Child Guidance Clinic. The head of every unit was a man. I looked around and acknowledged that she was right. Gender was completely outside of my way of looking.

Not too long after this the first feminist conference in family therapy happened at the Philadelphia Child Guidance Clinic. Marion Walters was one of the supervisors and Peggy Papp was teaching a course there. They invited Olga Silverstein and Betty Carter and convened the first conference.

It was a confusing time for me. I tried to respond to what I understood but I always needed to be reminded and there was so much I did not see. I also felt that I was being treated as 'the other' and at times a target. I have been treated as the other three times in my life. Once as a Jew. Then, when I was working in the African American community I was 'the other' because I was white. And then I was treated as 'the other' because I was a man.

When new ideas come into any field, they enter in a concentrated way, like point of a lance. New ideas require this. The work of Virginia Goldner, Rachel Hare-Mustin, Betty Carter and others completely altered how the field thought about issues of gender. And the feminist movement in family therapy continues.

In the beginning I thought the feminist group was into using ideas that were contrary to family therapy. But over years I began to realise that this was a blind-spot for me and that I needed to look at the ways in which I described families. For instance, I realised that I described enmeshment between mother and daughter, where from a feminist point of view it could be described as affiliation. I began to look at language all over again.

I have also revisited the idea of complementarity. When feminists questioned Bateson's idea of complementarity, they pointed out that society had been organised in ways to de-power women. That concept of feminism is clear to me, and I recognise how this means that the concept of complementarity needs to be modified. In some situations, it is not an appropriate way of understanding relationships between men and women – for instance in dysfunctional families and in cases of domestic violence. I can see how the concept of complementarity needs to include an understanding of the social de-powering of women. But I don't think the concept needs to be completely rejected.

I have tried to become more aware of issues of gender. My daughter has trained me, as has Pat, my wife, but I have come to it late. I don't resound to it. For my son and my daughter it is different. Their view of gender is completely different to my own. And my granddaughter will have a completely different view again of women and men. It is a topic about which I cannot add much except to acknowledge my difficulties.

I was born in 1970 just when the second wave of the women's movement was beginning here in the US. As I try to reflect over all that we have covered today in this conversation I realise that I was born almost fifty years after you were born, more than twenty years after you had travelled to Israel for the first time, and over ten years after you and others had begun what was to become the field of family therapy. Your influence on this field has been profound in so many ways. Could we perhaps end by considering some of the influences of the family therapy field that you think have been significant and will be enduring.

There are many. But perhaps one of the areas in which family therapy has made real inroads into the territory of organic psychiatry has been in work with poor families. Programs in poor communities based on systemic views of families have been very influential. This was, of course, one of the first areas which I wrote about many years ago. It was in the 1967 that I wrote 'Families of the Slums: an exploration of their structure and treatment.' The issues seem just as important now. How can we as therapists play a part in responding to the lives of those in poverty? How can we reverse the inertia and punitive attitudes that so often influence intervention in the lives of poor families? Just a few years ago, Patricia Minuchin, Jorge Colapinto and myself wrote a further book entitled, 'Working with families of the poor'. It explores how to tap into the healing possibilities that reside within poor families and communities. Family therapy approaches are having a significant influence on organisations that work with poor families. But we have so much still to do.

It has been a great pleasure and privilege to meet you and to talk about all that we have today, and I so look forward to the next time. Thank you so much.

3

Creating home

an interview with

Monica McGoldrick

Monica McGoldrick is the co-founder and director of the Family Institute of New Jersey, USA, and has over many years been a key figure in the field of family therapy. Monica has played a central role, as either author or editor, of a number of key texts, including: 'Women in Families: A framework for family therapy', 'Living Beyond Loss', 'Ethnicity and Family Therapy', 'Genograms in family assessment', as well as her most recent book, 'Revisioning Family Therapy: Race, culture and gender in clinical practice'. This interview took place in New Jersey. Cheryl White and David Denborough were present. David was the interviewer.

Over many years now you have been an influential figure in relation to encouraging the field of family therapy to engage with issues of culture. Could you explain why these issues have been important to you?

I suppose there are a number of different stories I could tell in relation to that question. For instance, I was raised by an African-American woman, Margaret Bush. She was the person I was closest to from the first days that I can remember until I left home. How could my relationship with her not have affected everything about me? How could that not be a part of what all this is about? And yet, I did not think this through until so many years later, when friends of mine, people of colour, began to raise with me questions about race and class privilege in this country. I am still trying to come to terms with what it meant as a white person in this country to be raised by an African-American nanny.

But there are other stories I could also tell in relation to your question, some of which may seem superficial, but I think they are part of the picture. When I left school I did not study therapy or psychology, I studied Russian and everything I could about the Soviet Union. I was in high school during the height of the Cold War, and I think I had a fantasy of trying to make some contribution in relation to bridging cultures. The safety of the world seemed to depend upon it. Then I ended up marrying a Greek man, and my engagement with the meaning of culture and how to bridge differences continued.

In coming to think about issues of culture, I had to come to terms with my own. I grew up with no knowledge whatsoever of what it meant to be Irish, so perhaps the biggest question I found myself asking was, how come we don't have an articulated culture? How come we're just regular? In time, of course, this led to other questions like where did we come from? And what does being Irish mean?

In a country like the US, immigrants have been pressed to lose their connection to their culture of origin in order to assimilate into the American way. In order to make a new secure life, many immigrants do let go of a great deal of their culture of origin. Perhaps it is then up to future generations to retrace the history, to reconnect with where their families come from. Perhaps this was true in relation to my family and that I was of the generation that was freed up to reconnect with our roots. What I think was also true is that in the 1970s and 1980s there was an increasing move towards reconnecting with culture. My experiences were a part of this broader process.

My experience of going to Ireland and getting in touch with my roots was utterly profound to me. I would find myself crying and not knowing from where the tears were coming. I don't know exactly what that means. Just as a lot was lost in the process of migration, a lot was also found in returning. I've never been the same since. When I came back to the US, I began to ask questions that never stop: what was your background, where did your people come from, where did they go, what did they do? It simply became clear to me that these questions mattered, but I don't know how to say more than that. It's not that I have a nostalgic sense of holding on to the past, I know that identity and culture are constantly changing, but something about our connection to our history and culture matters deeply to me, even if I cannot articulate it perfectly.

Although in my life there has been this long-term process of trying to understand issues of culture, coming to terms with race and racism has been more recent. I would have to say that my introduction to these issues was less as a collective process and more came about through my relationships with people of colour who were already part of my life. It has only been in the past few years that I have been realising how oblivious I have been to matters of racism and white privilege and just how wrong the social set-up is. This has significantly affected how I understand my life. At the same time, though, it has definitely been the hardest issue that I have had to try to figure out. I feel like I'm very much at the beginning of this process, as if I am just crawling out of a cave and beginning to say, okay, what on earth is happening here?

Were your explorations of gender issues in some way similar or different to these explorations of issues of culture and race?

As I was growing up I was as oblivious about gender as I was about culture, although that now seems so odd to say. My education in college and graduate school took place at very male dominated Ivy League schools. The gender ratio at my graduate school for instance was 16 to 1. There were almost no other women around and I missed everything about gender awareness that was occurring in the 1960s and 1970s. I think I was trying to accommodate to being a woman in a man's world and this was probably taking up all of my energy.

When issues of gender began to be talked about in the field of family therapy in the early 1980s, it was personally revolutionary. Actually it was very upsetting for quite a few years. It was really great to be a part of a movement of women, so I wasn't alone in the distress. But it was very upsetting because not only did I have to re-think all the theories which I had learnt, I also had to re-think every aspect of my family life, and of course once this process began there was no going back. The process of thinking through issues of gender and trying to create different ways of working certainly continues. It remains something I'm trying to work on and hope to get better at. We all continue to hope that the experiences of future generations of women will be better than those of the past.

As you have been talking I've been reminded of the title of your latest book, 'Revisioning family therapy'. It seems that there has been a parallel process of revisioning your own life. Can you say a little about how these two processes relate to one another?

It has been different depending upon the particular issue. Thinking through issues of culture was for me an exciting and enriching process. Assimilation robbed me of so much of who I am, and so engaging with issues of culture was very rewarding. Issues of gender, however, I found much more conflictual. There was no way of getting away from the fact that I was living in a family and a community and a society that is profoundly sexist. There were, of course, also tremendous gains. Instead of other women being competition, as they had been in my life previously, I came to see us as women being natural allies. And being surrounded by natural allies is a wonderful feeling. The race issue is harder, at least for me as a white woman. I feel that it's much harder to connect with other white people on these issues, and so I often feel quite isolated. It is so easy for us as white people to consider race and racism as peripheral issues, as if there is an option to look at them or not. But it's not an option. Not so long ago, issues of gender were seen as peripheral to family therapy – but gender issues are at the interior of every family and every structure, and most therapists would now make these links. Issues of race are also not an option, they are also ever present but in different ways. The profundity of segregation in terms of race makes it really hard for us as white people to begin to understand how race is constantly relevant in everyone's lives. The more I have tried to listen and think about the issue of race, and stay conscious of it, the bigger an issue I realise it is. And the more painful it is to me that I don't know how to connect with other white people in ways that will help move us along. In the field of family therapy we still hardly ever talk about issues of race, and when we do it's as if it is a very small thing. For instance, all too often, nobody's bothered if there's a room full of white people who are making all the decisions. There are levels of segregation of thought and practice that are so profound. I do feel that we are making some progress, but it is pretty slow.

As you say, there is a considerable distance between where we are now and where we would like to be. Could you talk a little more about from where the field has come? Can you speak about some of the considerations of history in the field of family therapy that you think are important, both in terms of gender and in terms of ethnicity and race?

I do feel that we've gotten to a place where our awareness of the significance of issues of gender, culture and race are not going to be left behind. They are seen as important now. Paying attention to these issues is beginning to be embedded in how we write, how we think, and how we ask questions. This, I think is great. Increasingly, within the field of family therapy, there is a multi-cultural set of perspectives. I think it will now be impossible to go back to the days when the white perspective was upheld as the only truth. This change has happened in twenty years, in a generation. There's a long way to go but it doesn't feel like we could lose the ground which we've gained. At least I really hope that's true.

In noticing how far we have come, I also think it's important to acknowledge that a lot of people have really committed themselves to making these changes to the field – and sometimes this has not been easy.

I recall reading your writing about some of the ways in which Virginia Satir was treated when she was one of the women at the forefront of family therapy many years ago. You so beautifully evoked what the effects might have been on her life of some of the confrontational ways in which senior men in the field related to her and her work. I remember you writing that at one point she ceased to attend public events in the US ...

Yes. There was a debate once between senior men entitled, 'Is Virginia Satir dangerous for family therapy?' I had always known this but somehow hadn't fully grasped the effects that such debates would have on the person they were about. The reason I find this story particularly significant is because when family therapy started, I would always have my Virginia Satir book in my pocket. Wherever she was presenting I would be in the audience. Whatever I had to do, I would always get there because listening to her was incredibly validating. Although I wouldn't have said this at the time, I now realise how much this had to do with gender. During those early years I experienced all the senior men as appallingly arrogant and dismissive. I was completely intimidated by them but also knew I would not want to work in the ways in which they did. Virginia Satir acted in such a different way, and yet in hindsight I see how badly she was treated by the field. It was years later when I met someone who knew her personally and she described how Virginia had lived her last years very isolated, that I came to re-think how we as a field had allowed this to happen. I still ask myself, 'How could I have been so oblivious as to not realise the effects on her?'

Can I ask you about the book 'Women in Families: A framework for family therapy' which you edited with Carol Anderson and Froma Walsh? If you were to try to convey to people who are new to the field, who now might be working with women and families, how the field is different now to when you put that book together, what would you say?

When we were working on that book in the late 1980s, in the field of family therapy there wasn't a category of women. There was no such thing as women in families, there were people in families. Families were seen simply as systems containing genderless people. Looking back, how could I have thought this? And how could everybody else have thought this?! Getting to the point of asking about women in families was very significant. Every question you ask a woman has a different meaning if you think that there are women in families, rather than genderless people in families. That book grew from the first women's conferences in family therapy that were held in 1984 and 1986 at a place called Stonehenge in Connecticut.

These meetings were extraordinary events. When I look back, there were the roots of dealing with race issues there which I didn't understand at the time. We invited women of colour and they mostly didn't come. One woman of colour who did attend kept speaking out about race issues, again and again. At the time I thought she was obnoxious. I thought, look we're barely getting gender issues raised here and in every conversation you just keep saying 'well how does race fit into this'. It was years until I realised, 'Oh no. What is the matter with me that I didn't understand?!' We had already published the first edition of the book 'Ethnicity and Family Therapy' and yet I was really stupid on issues of race then. I thought we could look at issues of gender without engaging with race. And I couldn't understand why so few women of colour wanted to come to Stonehenge, why they all turned us down. I felt we were trying so hard, we were holding a party and they were not even bothering to come. At those meetings I learned a lot about gender, and I have realised since that there was a lot more about gender, and race, that I didn't learn there.

Nonetheless, they were significant times. In 1984 I was forty-one. I was pregnant and I had been married for fifteen years. After the Stonehenge gatherings not one of us was ever the same again. After that first conference, there was never a place we went in the field that there wasn't a sense of our being allied in some way. It was like we made connections at that first conference that became friendships that we drew upon wherever we went. Nothing has been the same since. There were 40 women there and every one of them was spectacular. Every woman presented and it was like, oh my god, these people are incredible, what a field we have! The three days went on hopping until midnight – new people, new ideas, fresh insights. I can't convey what it was like – just spectacular, just amazing! It was really something.

Would you ever call another such meeting?

No. I wouldn't. It was the right time then. Because of all the enthusiasm after the first meeting we called a second one, but it was less successful. The second time around there was beginning to be a backlash about who was and wasn't invited; and about who the hell was Monica McGoldrick anyway to be creating this event. There was negativity of a sort that was completely absent at the first event. I thought to myself that I would never do that again. I never wanted to set up an exclusive club, just to start a network, and this had begun. Several years later, Betty Carter and I and some other women set up one international meeting in Copenhagen. It was an incredibly great meeting and we met a lot of women from different parts of the world, but again there was terrific backlash about us organising it so I wouldn't do that again either! Organising such events is a very complex process. I have no regrets being involved in the ways I was, but I wouldn't do any more!

To end, I'd really like to ask you about your work in relation to genograms, family life cycles and intergenerational connectedness. In some of your more recent writings you have described how these are linked to one of the tasks of therapy – to enable the creation of a sense of home. As you've talked today about retracing your roots in Ireland, or meeting with other women at the first Stonehenge gathering, it seems to me that you have been involved in creating many different sorts of homes. What does this metaphor mean to you and your work?

In 1985 I finished a book on genograms and their relevance for family therapists and immediately I began working on a different book, entitled 'You can go home again'. This was a book for regular people, not therapists and it took me many years to put it together. In the course of doing so I was going through my own transformation about the meaning of home. When I started the book I thought that home related to your family and your culture of origin. By the time I finished it, I realised that home also had to do with race and class and gender and a sense of belonging in ways that are so much larger than family. But of course it is all related.

Let me give you an example. My mother wasn't a very good mother. She wasn't affectionate and she was extremely critical. For a long time I judged her very harshly for all that she didn't do, and all she did wrong. By the mid 1980s, after the first Stonehenge meeting, I was in the midst of struggling to come to terms with issues of gender (I still am!). But I had spent a lot of time trying to get my relationship with my own mother to a better place. It was only through engaging with issues of gender that I could understand more of the context of my mother's life. It was only looking at the broader issues that I began to realise the ways her life had been affected by gender. Her options for life had been erased due to gender and she had also lost her culture through the broader immigration experience. Thinking about my mother's life in these ways was like coming to see her in a different light. I came to see how she had already lost home before I was in the picture. By the time I finished, 'You Can Go Home Again', I dedicated the book to my mother.

Now I see creating home as involving finding a way that we can all belong. It's like creating ways of understanding our lives that include all of everyone's experience. It's like creating a container that's big enough for everyone. Where once I saw the process of going home as retracing our roots, reconnecting with family, now I see it as all of that and more. It is about creating an awareness that we are all connected. It's about continuing to revision our lives and the fields in which we work, so that they are expansive enough to affirm everyone's differing perspectives of class, race, sexuality, culture and gender. That's a different kind of home, and it's the one in which I want to live.

4

Systemic practice

an interview with

Gianfranco Cecchin

The Milan approach to family therapy was developed in the late 1960s early 1970s by Mara Selvini Palazzoli, Luigi Boscolo, Gianfranco Cecchin and Giuliana Prata. From the late 1970s Mara Selvini Palazzoli and Giuliana Prata went on to conduct further research, while Luigi Boscolo and Gianfranco Cecchin continued to conduct family therapy training and to consult families. In this interview, which took place in Oslo, Norway, at the Family Therapy World Congress, Gianfranco Cecchin speaks about how the very influential Milan approach has continually evolved over the years.

Could you possibly trace some of the challenges and dilemmas that you were facing when you first began to develop what has come to be known as the 'Milan' school of family therapy?

There has been a continual evolution of the work of the so-called Milan school. In the beginning, we were utilising ideas that derived from Palo Alto (Jackson, Haley, Watzlawick and Bateson). The key aspect of their work that influenced ours was the emphasis of looking at everything through the lens of relationships. Along with others at that time, we were trying to move away from the idea of individual diagnosis and towards a focus on family relationships and the ways in which family systems worked.

In a family, everything happens in relation to something else. If something happens with one family member, then there must be consequences in the lives of the others. No human being acts in isolation. We are always acting in relation to others.

Having decided that this emphasis on relationship and family systems fitted for us, we then began to explore each sort of action that was taking place between family members. We began to look at every action and to translate them into what they meant in terms of relationship. We would make hypotheses about this. For example, we would take a particular action of a family member and try to determine whether he or she was acting 'for' another family member, or whether he or she was perhaps acting in this way because another family member was telling them to do so.

Unfortunately, I believe we got stuck around some of these issues. Our hypotheses tended to describe everything we saw as a power game. We saw families as if they were a political field in which all the parties were trying to control each other. What this meant in practice was that we would often end up focusing our thinking about a family around the questions, 'Who, in this family, is in control? Who is more powerful? Who is in charge?' Even the symptoms were seen as part of the power play. We may have hypothesised that the child was displaying certain symptoms in such a way so that they could control the parents. Or that the grandmother was doing something in order to control everyone.

At that time, similar ideas were also being talked about by others. Even Jay Haley, in talking about power relationships, routinely made out as if family relationships were about a struggle for power. Whether it was parents claiming power over the children, the children having power over the parents, or the husband having power over the wife, I believe we became stuck as we focused on and really invented stories of power and control. Even the language we used was informed by these ideas. We would describe family members as making a manoeuvre, or being resistant, or provoking us. In hindsight, even the word neutrality, which we developed to describe the position of the therapist, was evoking a language of warfare. It described that we as therapists were to remain neutral, that we would not side with one warring party against another.

We also understood the therapeutic relationship in terms of power relationships. We believed that the therapist needed to 'control' the relationship. As therapists we would say things such as 'you have to come for ten sessions' or alternatively 'all the family members will have to attend. If you don't attend it will mean you are trying to put us down.' We believed that if the therapist did not have control over the therapeutic relationship that therapy was impossible.

During this time you were also developing particular therapeutic interventions that were to significantly influence the field. Would you like to talk a little about these?

Well, we were making hypotheses about ways in which the family system was organised and these hypotheses were often about the power games we believed we were witnessing. We were then inventing methods to break these power games. One of these methods involved paradoxical intervention, while another involved prescribing some rituals for family members to conduct without explaining what they were doing. We believed that if the family members performed these rituals it would be likely to result in changes in the family system.

Can you say a little more about paradoxical intervention?

Mostly what we were concerned about were 'positive descriptions' – making positive connotations of the system the way it was. For example, when people would come to us with problems that they had been unable to change, we would sometimes strongly recommend that they didn't change. We would state that we believed that change in fact would be dangerous. We would state that we believed that what the family was doing was actually the very best thing they could do in relation to the problem. If they did anything else, something could occur that may not be desirable. We would say that we didn't understand what was going on yet and that we recommended they didn't make any changes at all until we understood the dangers involved. These paradoxical interventions would often result in changes taking place in the system.

As I understand it, you have often written about how your work and thinking has been transformed by feedback you have received from students. Would you like to speak a little about this?

When we trained students and tried to teach them to do what we were doing with the families, they were very interested in asking questions about us. Why do you do what you do? Why do you say that? Why are you nice to these people and not to these other ones? Why do you speak with these people and not to these people? They were more interested in the behaviour of the therapist, rather than the behaviour of the people coming for therapy.

Their questions invited us to see that we as therapists had a lot of set ideas, and to look at how these ideas were influencing what we were doing. If a therapist has a certain scheme of mind then this influences what he or she sees. When we saw some students work, they did not hypothesise about family power struggles in the ways in which we were, and this enabled them to see other descriptions. We came to realise that we had organised ourselves to see power games and therefore we saw them all the time.

This led to an important shift. Perhaps families did not come together with the most important question being 'who is more powerful?', but instead they come together just to make sense of each other. Rather than there being a struggle of power, there might be a struggle to make sense of the relationships. This very useful step meant that we began to see people wanting to be sure that what they said made sense to others. We began to see people who were very happy because they had come to common understandings – they agreed on what made sense to them. And we began to witness how people sometimes get totally confused as they struggle to make sense of each other's realities.

We have now come to be interested in how people build their stories, and not necessarily stories that are connected with power games. We have come to see that the power game is just one of many stories. There are many stories in therapy and making changes to these stories can bring effects. We are interested in asking questions about 'How did this story come up?' 'Who invented this story first?' 'Why is this story interesting to one person and not to the other?'

What about some of the key principles that the Milan team introduced to the field? How are these used today?

There are a number of principles of systemic thinking that still very much inform the work that we do. The influence of positive connotation is still important. When looking at a system, we try to look at what is right rather than looking at what is wrong. The traditional way was to see what was wrong, what was violent, what was bad, what was pathological, what was stupid, what was incompetent. Instead we said, let us look at what is right. Even in the worst of situations do you see anything right? If a system is alive, if it is in front of you to witness, then something must be working.

Another principle is that human systems naturally tend towards happiness and to keep low the level of cruelty that all human beings harbour within themselves. There are many impediments to this tendency to happiness and to contain cruelty and we believe our job as therapists is to remove these impediments. We are not helping the people to be happy in themselves, but we are helping to get rid of what makes it difficult for them to be happy. What makes it difficult is usually something that was invented by the system itself. Impediments we see as being within the relationships, rather than something to do with bigger power systems. This is one idea about which we have a lot of discussion with other people! Some people say we must work at the political level – if we change the political situation then people will become happier. But that's a political job and we are therapists. Our theory is that even if you are in an unjust situation you can be happy if the little system you create around you makes sense to you. This is not like saying we ought to do nothing about the broader issues – we can work at the political level. But that is not a condition to make the micro-system one that can bring happiness. The micro-system can make happiness possible even in very difficult circumstances. As systemic therapists we believe it is our role to address the impediments within the family system.

And what about some of the particular therapeutic practices that the Milan team originated?

We have always maintained the idea of circular questioning which was one of the first methods we developed. Systemic theory states that human systems are always in a state of flux. They are always moving and are never perfect. It is when a system becomes stuck, when it becomes predictable, that someone develops symptoms. As systemic therapists, we are interested in eliciting differences that can move a system along. Circular questioning involves eliciting family members' opinions regarding various sorts of differences. Questions might focus around differences in the perceptions between family members, or differences between what was happening in the past and in the present, or speculations about what might be different in the future. There is a whole range of sorts of questions about differences that can be asked. Through the questioning itself changes to the family system can occur.

A further consistent strand has been a commitment to being reflective. We always have people behind the mirrors talking about what is going on. We have always been asking questions but now we look for different things. We began to try to find out what is in the head of therapists. What kind of lenses do we have? What affect are our ideas having on what we see? When we have ideas and we take some initiative, what affect does this have? What are the set of prejudices that we have now in relation to what we see?

What are some of the issues that you feel practitioners are trying to grapple with in family therapy at present?

An issue that I am very interested in involves the question of diagnosis. I am presenting at this conference on the topic 'Can we survive without diagnosis?' My idea is that diagnosis is good for big insurance companies. They need to know what they are doing in order to function, but the ways we work at the micro level, in talking with individuals, we don't need diagnosis. Diagnosis is good for others, but not for family therapists. Others may need to make diagnosis – for funding, for statistics, for a whole range of reasons, but we do not!

There seems to be a healthy diversity of perspectives in this conference. Is that your sense?

Yes, because there are so many lenses through which we can view families. Everybody is facing the same issues from different angles. I think this diversity is good. In some circles, there is a question about whether systemic family therapy and narrative therapy are in contradiction. I don't see it that way at all. Systemic thinking is about looking at the ways in which human beings are organised and people have different understandings about this. To me, narratives hold systems together. Narratives are the stories that keep systems together. There is not a major difference. We are giving different emphases. Narrative is a beautiful word. We all depend on stories, we come out of stories, we build stories together.

My feeling is that all family therapists are still the minority view in the health system and we probably always will be. Basically, in my view, the mental health system is preoccupied with organising conformity, and this is a great danger for the future. So many therapists are now looking for simple solutions and turning to medications. There is a growing obedience to the bigger health system. I am very interested in what *all* family therapists can do, whatever their perspective, to reinvigorate curiosity in these situations and in institutions.

This idea of a therapy informed by curiosity was another of your significant contributions ...

It was a very simple idea. In our work we always wait and seek out something unusual, something different. Every human being is always slightly irreverent. There is always something unusual to discover and this discovery often brings change. Human systems are in permanent evolution. It is the difference that brings movement. It is when the system gets stuck that a malaise happens. So that is when therapists enter, when the system is stuck. We believe we ought to be looking for the elements that can help the system make steps forward. We are always curious to find them!

Thank you Gianfranco, it's been a great pleasure speaking with you and I look forward to hearing your presentation.

5

Feminist reflections on family therapy and working on the issue of men's violence

an interview with

Kerrie James

Kerrie James is the Clinical Director of Relationships Australia, NSW. As a couple and family therapy practitioner, Kerrie has presented and published both in Australia and overseas in the area of gender, supervision, attachment and therapeutic practice. She was recently awarded the Special Contributions to Australian Family Therapy Award by the Board of the Australian and New Zealand Journal of Family Therapy.

The following interview took place at the Family Therapy World Congress in Oslo where Kerrie was presenting with Beth Seddon on the topic 'Men's experience of their violence towards female partners – implication of research finding for family/couple therapy'. In this interview Kerrie describes the influence that feminist thinking has had on the Australian family therapy scene.

Would it be okay to start by describing some of the contexts that led to the early discussions around feminist issues in family therapy in Australia?

I hope my memory serves me correctly! I remember coming back to Australia from North America, in the late 1970s early 1980s and realising that the Australian family therapy field was very much dominated by male psychiatrists. It wasn't substantially different in the US at the time either, but there were some conversations happening about issues of gender. A colleague and I, Gill Calvert, then wrote a piece for a publication in an international family therapy newsletter. We called the piece something like 'What happened to women in family therapy?' When this piece was published, Michael White, whom I didn't know at the time, came across it and asked if we'd be interested in republishing it in the Australia and New Zealand Journal of Family Therapy, of which he was the editor at that time. We also talked about creating a kind of regular column in the Journal so that there could be an ongoing debate about feminist issues in family therapy.

So these were the first few steps of my involvement in these issues. Then in 1984 the national family therapy conference was to be held in Canberra. The year before, a 'women in family therapy' meeting had been held in Adelaide and it was decided that it would become a tradition to hold a separate women's meeting before each national conference. This was pretty contentious in the early years with various men coming into the women's meetings and sitting in the front row! When it came to the Canberra conference, the organisers decided that they didn't want a separate women's meeting because they feared that it would distract from the main conference.

I remember having discussions with Gill and other people and we decided that the only way to really address the issue was to present a plenary on why women needed to meet separately at the main conference. I can't remember whether we came up with the idea or whether the organisers said, 'Why don't you do a plenary?'. Anyway, I ended up doing the plenary. It was an extraordinary conference and very contentious on various issues but there were also a whole range of people who were very supportive.

I gave the plenary entitled 'Breaking the chains of gender'. It focused on gender issues in family therapy and their relevance to our work as clinicians. I spoke about how there was so much fantastic work happening around the world about issues of gender at the time and asked why there wasn't a discussion about these issues in family therapy in Australia. I tried to explain why we wanted to have a separate space for women's voices and asked why there was so much opposition to this idea.

I remember at the time there was a whole group of female psychiatrists sitting to my right, not looking very supportive. It wasn't just a split between men and women. It was really a split between people who were more consciously aware of gender issues and those who were frightened that engaging with these issues, particularly if it took the form of a separate women's meeting, would somehow split the field.

There was a group of 'women in family therapy' in Sydney who were very strong and there was similar group in Adelaide. The tradition of women's meetings prior to national conferences has continued to this day. In the 1980s there were also a number of international conferences for women in family therapy. The only one that I attended was in Copenhagen in 1991 and it was a phenomenal experience, as it always seems to be when women come together around these sorts of issues. Of course, issues of diversity between women are so important that it is impossible to refer to gender issues in any exclusive way.

Looking back, for a time there I felt positioned in Australian family therapy as the voice of women! But I was doing a lot of other things at the same time!

What were some of the issues that feminist women were trying to raise at that time?

I think the main issue that I was trying to raise, and I wrote about this in a paper with Deborah McIntyre called 'The reproduction of families, the social role of family therapy?' which was published in the Journal of Marital and Family Therapy, was that the way of approaching gender issues in family therapy was reasonably superficial. We felt that it was important not to simply consider issues of gender in the context of the family, but also in the broader social context. We were challenging structural ideas that asserted that, in order to effect change in the family, it would be sufficient to involve the father in the family. These ideas ignored a socio-political context that limited and influenced the ways in which fathers are involved in families. We were trying to say that family therapy occurs in a socio-political context of power inequity between men and women in terms of wealth, status and social standing which impacted on family relationships and which had to be addressed in therapy. Along with many others in family therapy, both in Australia and the USA, we were seeking to bring the ideas of feminism into a traditional, male dominated field. Despite the systemic thinking of converted psychiatrists who had rejected psycho-dynamic models and adopted systemic models, they themselves had no awareness of their own positions of power and how they viewed and treated female colleagues and women in families.

We also pointed out that family therapy had been going on for fifteen years and yet there was very little written on issues of domestic violence, child sexual assault, or child abuse. It was as if these issues didn't exist. When these issues were written about there was a host of problems with victim blaming, psychologising, and avoiding issues of power and responsibility. That led Laurie MacKinnon and me to write about the myths expounded in family therapy publications about child sexual abuse. Interestingly, the areas which the feminist movement outside of family therapy was addressing in relation to families, such as violence, abuse, housework, childcare, were completely absent in the theoretical writings published in major journals in family therapy. We were asking what this silence was about, and wondering who was being silenced in the process.

Even today in the mainstream journals there is not a lot of attention paid to these issues, but you cannot say that it is the same as it once was. There has been a huge shift in thinking in the field and a lot of space is now available for all sorts of discussions about oppression, justice, abuse and diversity. This is incredibly pleasing and gratifying, because it certainly wasn't like that through most of the 1980s, except for a few women such as the Women's Project at the Ackerman, Virginia Goldner, Rachel Hare-Mustin, Judith Myers-Avis to name a few, and some men, like Morris Taggart.

Can you say a little bit about some of the important steps that have enabled these issues to come into the focus of the field?

It's hard to know how it has all happened except that struggles around issues of race have been really significant in influencing the development of feminist theory over the years. Gradually the voices of marginalised women have become more and more prominent – starting out with a critique and a challenge to the dominant view that was being expressed within feminism. I believe the debate around black/white relations in North America, in third world countries and within Australia, has been as significant an influence as the issue of gender has been. Gay and lesbian challenges to commonly held views of what is family have also been influential, as have the voices of other marginalised groups. All these voices have thoroughly challenged conceptions of family, family relations and family therapy and this has been very significant. In Australia, the work of the Dulwich Centre has also played a major role in bringing these issues into the family therapy arena.

How have these discussions led to the development of feminist practices in the field of family therapy? What are some of the considerations that influence a feminist family therapy practice?

In my own practice, I am interested in looking at how issues of inequity or abuses of power are experienced and expressed in relationships, and the relevance of therapy in making space for unexpressed and unspoken experience. In this way, therapy itself is about issues of equity and fairness, how these can be raised and addressed, and how people can make changes. Therapy is often about finding leverages for change so that people who don't have a voice, who have been relatively powerless, can find ways to facilitate changes in their lives. Having said all of that, I believe that most models or approaches to family therapy can encompass these kinds of perspective. It mostly depends on the consciousness or the values of the therapist. I don't think that it can be said that there is a feminist family therapy model or practice. Feminist ideas infiltrate our lives, our experiences and our teaching.

Can you speak about the work that you are presenting on here at this conference, the directions that your feminist informed practice has taken you?

Certainly. A few years ago now, Beth Seddon, National Director, Relationships Australia; Dr Jac Brown, University of Macquarie; Dr Michael Wearing, University of New South Wales; and I, began working on a research project in relation to how men experience and construct their own violence against their partners. Our organisations have struggled for years about what are appropriate services to offer these men. The New South Wales Government has taken a position of refusing to fund any services for these men. While we have not done this, we have been determined to find ways to offer a service that acknowledges the seriousness of the issue and does not therapise something that shouldn't be therapised.

When we received this money to research men's experience, we were already running programs for men and began to conduct quantitative and qualitative research. We interviewed about twenty-four men and then analysed the transcripts of these interviews. We picked out the common themes that men were describing and tried to account for the commonalities and then we tried to account for the differences. The results have been intriguing.

The results could basically be broken into two groups. One group of men (whom we went on to describe as the 'tyrants') described their violence as something they did to get their own way. They were quite conscious of this. They spoke of how they used violence when they felt angry and frustrated and when they were thwarted. They experienced being in control and planning the violence. Then we had another group of men whose experiences were different (we called these men the 'exploders'). They experienced their violence as out of control, as coming upon them. They experienced themselves as losing control. In order to try to account for these differences we looked at the men's family of origin and the kinds of relationships they were in.

The relationship differences were very significant. Those men in the group we called the 'exploders' were generally in relationships with women whom they had believed they were rescuing at the beginning of the relationships. They saw the women as having problems and that they were hero-like, coming along to rescue them from these problems. When the women started to do well, feel more secure in the relationships and stand up to the man or challenge him in some way, the men felt betrayed and in some way saw themselves as victims. All of the exploder men were rescuers, and all of them saw themselves as victims in the relationship in some way.

All of the men in the group we described as the 'tyrants', however, appeared to have married women who had sussed out the men's violence pretty quickly and had taken a one-down position in relation to it. The 'exploders' were in relationships in which the women fought with the men and the men just 'lost it' and fought back. In the 'tyrant' group, however, the men were more dominant. When we looked at their relationships they looked like bullies to us.

When we looked at the men's families of origin, we found that there were predominantly three different types of family that they came from. Eighteen out of the twenty-four men interviewed had all experienced severe abuse as children. Interestingly, of the 130 men who had filled out initial questionnaires, only a much smaller percentage talked about abuse in their families of origin. It was only when we started the qualitative interviews that we realised to what extent many of the men initially minimised or denied abuse in their family of origin but by the end of the interview were describing quite explicit abuse. I guess what this demonstrates is that you can't just ask men straight up about whether they came from abusive backgrounds because their experiences are probably not something that they will understand to be abusive. Abusive treatment to boys in these generations of men was so taken for granted that they don't see themselves as having experienced abuse. Often this contributes to them not seeing their own actions as abusive.

We hope that this study may assist us in identifying risk factors and protective factors. There are also interesting implications for therapeutic work with men in relation to who to work with, who not to work with, and what kinds of approaches may be most useful for what kinds of violence. The men who have a more controlling paradigm may fit much better with socio-educational models, whereas others may be helped much more by therapy. I think this kind of research will open up a lot of possibilities.

What would you see as the current challenges, dilemmas or exciting developments in the field of family therapy?

I think family therapy has a bit of an identity issue at present. It's blurring a lot into individual therapy and the focus on relationships is potentially being lost. I think the challenge for family therapists is to stay focused on relationships and to stay working with families. As practitioners get experienced, they often move into private practice and start seeing couples or working long-term with individuals. This almost inevitable process can mean that we lose our cutting edge in working with families. If people do start focusing more on individual therapy, then I don't think this should be called family therapy. There are plenty of spaces to discuss individual therapy. I'd like to see us stay focused on working with relationships, particularly for children's sake, as I really believe that work with families has a lot to offer.

I also think that those working with the families who are experiencing the effects of poverty and multiple disadvantage ought to be getting more support from others in the field. They need to be getting supervision, recognition and support. We should be developing training contexts to assist these practitioners to stay focused on working with these families and to develop new ideas. I think this is quite a challenge for the field!

6

African-American experience and the healing of relationships

an interview with

Kenneth V. Hardy

Kenneth V. Hardy is a well known and widely respected family therapist who lives in New York where he works at the Ackerman Institute for the Family. A seasoned clinician, he has published extensively in professional journals, created numerous professional videotapes, and sits on several editorial boards including the Journal of Marital and Family Therapy, Family Science Review, Family Therapy Networker and Family Process. This interview took place in New York City. Cheryl White and David Denborough were the interviewers.

Could we start perhaps with how it is that you came to be engaged with the field of family therapy?

I grew up in Pennsylvania in Philadelphia as the oldest of six siblings. Throughout my childhood there was significant emphasis placed on the importance of the family. My maternal great-grandmother lived with us until I was a junior in college. She was the granddaughter of a slave and I can't think of another person who's had a more profound influence on me. She taught me what can't be learnt from books. She told me stories about humanity and human beings, about the potential for kindness and the potential for inhumanity. I heard so much from her about the ugliness of slavery and the impact it had on her parents' life and my parents' life.

I knew very early on what I wanted to do with my life. I had an insatiable yearning for some greater understanding of what we had become as a people and why. When I was exposed to the whole area of psychotherapy, I found that there was some attention being paid to issues of poverty, race and ethnicity but only in superficial ways. This was when I got excited about family therapy. I think my own family predisposed me to be interested in this area.

As an African-American working in a field that is dominated by white people and white values, I've had to get in there, step in the mud, make mistakes, have people laugh at me, feel ashamed and just continue. There certainly wasn't a manual as to how to act and I had to endure the humiliation of not really knowing how to act in the white professional world.

One of the reasons why there are so few people of colour, so few African-Americans in the field of family therapy, is because family therapy has been a somewhat marginalised discipline in comparison to mainstream psychology or psychiatry. It's very difficult for those of us who have membership in devalued and marginalised groups to invest heavily in a profession that's in some ways marginalised and devalued. There's something about getting educated and finding the right job as an African-American that's supposed to be freeing. There are meanings involved in employment and education for African-American people that are different than for white Americans.

For African-Americans to engage with family therapy it requires us to practice unrequited love. It requires people of colour to love family therapy more than it seems to love us! The curriculum in universities is not designed to look at marginalised experiences so I had a lot of discouragement along the way. I recall in graduate school a professor saying to me, 'Maybe you should look at some other area because white families probably won't think about going to see a black therapist, and a lot of black people don't believe in therapy'. I had my own ideas about this however, and if I had my life over again I would live it the same way. I'd be a family therapist.

Much of your work has involved trying to articulate the skills and steps required in healing relationships, especially those affected by differences in power. Can you speak a little about this?

In terms of healing any relationship, I believe there has to be some willingness to look at dynamics of power. Power is an integral part of our relationships and until that's acknowledged it is often very difficult to move forward. Once there is an acknowledgement of the relevance of addressing issues of power, I am interested in drawing distinctions between those who are privileged and those who are subjugated. I think that while both have responsibilities in relation to healing relationships, the responsibilities are not equal. In situations where a relationship has broken down,

I've attempted to define what some of the different tasks are for those in privileged positions and those in subjugated positions. Of course, I don't think these categories of privilege and subjugation are absolute. The same person can occupy positions in different categories on different issues – e.g. culture, gender, class, sexuality. And yet I have found it helpful to try to articulate what the different responsibilities might be for those in privileged positions and those in subjugated positions in order for relationships to be healed.

One of the first responsibilities for the privileged is to overcome mistaken notions about equality and inequality. I believe it's customary for the privileged to just assume that everyone and everything is equal. One of the privileges of the privileged is to be able to be oblivious to the life experiences of the subjugated. I don't believe healing can take place in a context where the privileged have not come to terms with the existence of inequality. Not only must the privileged acknowledge the existence of marginalisation, they must find some way to appreciate the inequality and the suffering of the subjugated.

There is also a critical distinction that has to be made between intentions and consequences. In my experience, the privileged almost always deal in the realm of intentions, while the subjugated almost always deal in the realm of consequences. Often this means that there can't be a dialogue between the privileged and the subjugated because their reference points are so different. It's important to realise that you can have pure intentions that render very damaging consequences. In order for healing to take place, the privileged must stop routinely using their position to clarify their intentions in ways that disregard the very real effects of their actions.

Furthermore, it amazes me when people of privilege say, 'I tried to reach out to this group of people but they were so hostile and angry that I just can't do it anymore'. I think that such statements are an expression of privilege. They are a cop-out. I get frustrated because I think that sometimes privileged folks, whether it's men, or white people or heterosexuals, seem to require a manual before they will take action. They want to know how to approach these issues in 'the right way', a way that involves the least amount of risk to them. Perhaps they are used to being guided through life, perhaps they are used to being able to follow guidelines that are set up to enable them to progress through life. This is not true for people in subjugated positions. We are familiar with the feeling of not knowing what to do. We are used to facing hostility and anger when we step into unfamiliar territory. If relationships across difference are to be healed then people of privilege cannot turn away at their first experience of rejection or hostility. If we, as members of marginalised groups, gave up when we experienced hostility, we would get nowhere in life.

For the subjugated, there are different responsibilities. The most important of these is to find some way to regain one's voice. One cannot experience domination and subjugation and retain the whole strength of one's voice, it quickly becomes compromised. I think that there has to be a concerted effort to regain that which has been taken away, that which has been lost. There have to be steps taken to reclaim one's voice, one's heritage, one's history.

I think another major task for the subjugated is to find a way to have some willingness to allow the privileged to come to terms with their participation in injustice. It is very difficult for gay and lesbian people to sit there and watch a heterosexual get agitated or upset in relation to issues of heterosexual dominance, because most gay and lesbian people know that if heterosexual people get angry it can culminate in some form of violence. It is very difficult for African-Americans or people of colour to sit there and watch a white person get agitated and upset, because we know that horrible things often happen when white people get mad. It is very difficult for the poor person to sit there when a very wealthy person gets upset, because they know the person with wealth will have the resources to get them withdrawn from the situation if they decide they have had enough of the uncomfortableness.

I think that part of the socialisation process for subjugated peoples is to be trained into finding ways to take care of the privileged. That is just a part of our experience. You look at those who shine shoes in the airports, those who make the beds up in hotels, and those who drive cabs – they are all people from subjugated groups. One of the dominant stories of our lives involves taking care of the privileged, doing this well and doing it in self-compromising ways. When we are trying to address injustices in our relationships this is something the subjugated have to come to terms with. We have to deal with our tendency to instantly take care of people from privileged positions. We have to enable privileged people to engage with these issues and come up with their own responses. Members of subjugated groups must find ways through this without responding to privileged people's uncomfortableness in self-compromising ways.

The other experience that the subjugated have to come to terms with is to find some channel for rage. For many people, experiences of subjugation and domination are accompanied by rage. Rage is not anger which can be an immediate response to a particular situation. Rage is historical and it's tied to experiences of domination and subjugation. There is nothing episodic about rage; it's long-term. I believe that subjugated people's experience of rage can contribute to the short life expectancy of our people. We need to try to understand our rage and to find ways to use it which are constructive both for individuals and our communities.

We have to find better ways to help those who are subjugated to channel their rage because the alternative scares me. In some ways I can relate to the stereotypic menace to society on the streets of New York who is mean and angry and waiting for his next victim. Sometimes I think that the difference between my life and his may not be as great as it seems. Maybe the difference is that I have found some way to channel my rage. This discussion is a chance to channel rage. I have speech, I have writing, I have my work with people. These are all ways in which I can engage with my rage that are not destructive of myself or others.

In Australia at the moment there is considerable discussion about the place of apologies in relation to addressing historical injustices. What is your view in relation to this?

There are three key steps the privileged can take in relation to past injustice. Firstly, there has to be a meaningful acknowledgement of the injustice. Secondly, there has to be an apology for the injustice done. And thirdly, there has to be a request for forgiveness. With anything short of this it's very difficult to heal.

You have a large group of African-Americans in this country who remain very angry, in a way that white people can't understand, because there's been no formal acknowledgement and apology in relation to slavery. I think an apology would go a long way towards collective healing. And yet somehow we haven't got to that point. There are examples of ways of relating to past horrors that we can learn from. You can go to Washington DC, for example, and hear about the horrors of the Holocaust but there are no similar museums dedicated to honouring the massacres and genocide that happened on this soil. To this day we have the most alarming rates of alcoholism and suicide on most First Nations' reservations and the reaction from the mainstream is, 'Why won't those damn Indians stop drinking?'. People don't say, 'Well that's because their whole lives, and their children's lives, and their parents' lives and their grandparents' lives, have been assaulted by this country'. You don't hear those parts of the story. I think an apology to the indigenous peoples of this land, and a formal apology in relation to slavery would go a long way towards healing the psyche of this country. Clearly there would need to be powerful acts of acknowledgement around this apology, and a request for forgiveness. If this occurred I think it could be transformative for this nation.

How do these sorts of considerations translate into your work as a therapist with families?

Part of my frustration with our field is that we seem so determined to locate human suffering narrowly while ignoring broader ecological perspectives. In family therapy we pride ourselves on having a systemic understanding of problems, that we need to look not just at the individual but at the whole family. But in some ways this is still very narrow, because the family exists in a broader socio-cultural context. Because I am interested in the effect of this socio-cultural context on those with whom I meet, I've had colleagues seriously say to me, 'you're not a therapist, you're a sociologist', or, 'you're an anthropologist'. This is not an insult to me. I'm pleased to hear such remarks. What they mean to me is that in therapy, I'm always looking for connections between what's happening in this micro-systemic relationship and how it's tied to one's experiences in macro systems of culture.

Just a couple of days ago we had a Russian couple come in who had recently emigrated to the USA. They have a very volatile relationship and are in the process of destroying each other. Small things trigger huge arguments, such as when she says to him, 'Can you take your shoes off when you're walking on the carpet?' How are we as therapists to approach such a circumstance? We could focus on their communication and their need for anger management, but I'd prefer to explore what it means to be a Russian who lives in the United States. I don't know what it's like to be a Russian who lives in this country but I do know what it's like to have membership in a group which relentlessly receives very powerful messages about being 'less than'. My understanding of this couple dynamic is that some piece of what we're dealing with is within their relationship, some piece has to do with some critical, domineering parenting pattern, but another part of it has to do with the way they feel very profoundly disrespected in this society as Russians. There is a way in which they have been so profoundly devalued that it has altered their understandings about how to act in order to achieve the respect of each other.

Most of the ways that people approach therapy don't even begin to consider matters of ethnicity and culture of origin. Most therapies don't even begin to wonder about the impact of the minute everyday cultural practices on the experiences of individuals and families. I want to expand the dialogue so that therapy is not seen as being restricted to conversations about a particular problem that someone may be experiencing. In society, race, class, gender, sexual orientation and other dimensions of diversity are always a part of our interactions. There should be some opportunity to talk about these issues in the therapy room because otherwise the conversations may not be acknowledging significant realms of experience.

I couldn't trust a therapist I was seeing who didn't talk about my experiences as an African-American. If I couldn't do that it wouldn't be therapy worth believing in. Being African-American is such a core piece of my identity. And yet I wouldn't expect my therapist to raise the issue for the sake of raising it. Instead, I'd expect him or her to be a good seamstress in the ways they assisted me to see how the issues of my life are stitched together, how my experiences of life are linked to broader histories and the wider ecology.

Can you expand on the metaphors of ecology and how such a metaphor influences your thinking and your work?

One of the struggles in my life is to resist the temptation and seduction of simplicity. There are lots of opportunities in a technologically advanced society to make our lives simpler. Yet what feels more meaningful for me is to keep struggling to understand my life and the lives of others in all their wonderful complexity. My own life, in hundreds of ways each day, is shaped by relations of gender, race and religion. How I understand a particular situation is influenced by so many histories, it's just that we are not trained to see this. We are not encouraged to make the links between how we understand our lives and the broader relationships of culture, gender, class and sexuality. In fact, this is often actively discouraged to the point that we cease to look for or to realise what significant factors these broader relations of power have in our daily lives. Segregated thinking is such a cancer in our society.

Let me give you an example from my own life. If I was to measure myself against a psychological scale in relation to paranoia, I think I would rate so highly that I would be off the scale! Yet I think it would be a mistake to interpret such a result as simply an indication of my craziness. When I get stopped by a policeman because of my membership of a group that's systematically targeted, paranoia is a logical response. What is seen through one lens as psychological paranoia, in another can be seen as a logical result of discrimination and racism.

In this context, ahistorical, non-ecological approaches miss so much. If I was to understand my experience by thinking, 'if only I could trust more, if only I could take a pill to get rid of this paranoia that is inside of me', then I would miss the opportunity to take meaningful action to challenge the relations of power that are discriminating against me. I think therapy – that is to say therapy built on ecological understandings, that makes the links between people's experiences of life and the power relations of the society in which they live – goes hand-in-hand with activism.

There are those therapists who believe family therapy has gone too far in terms of its involvement in human rights issues. They say we can't be an 'Amnesty International' for families, that we should just help couples navigate the stresses of their lives. But from my point of view, we have an obligation to change the world. Our job is to serve families, indeed to serve *all* families, not just the wealthy and those who speak a common language, but those who aren't even sure what language they speak. It's our responsibility to make the links between the issues families are facing and broader relations of power. And it's our responsibility to take some action in relation to redressing injustices in the culture in which we live.

One of the realms of injustice that I know you are constantly speaking about involves the effects of the criminal justice system on families and communities of colour. Can you say a little about this?

Even if you go to places in the USA that don't have a high African-American population, when you look inside the prisons there you find disproportionate numbers of African-Americans because they're shipped in from other states. The current over policing and imprisonment of African-American people is a form of ongoing colonisation. In my more melodramatic moments I say it's the new slavery. We've replaced chains and plantations with bars and razor wire. In some ways the phenomena is exactly the same.

The great sadness is that the general population assumes that it's just, that 'they wouldn't be there if they didn't deserve to be'. But the laws in this country aren't equally applied. If you look at those who receive the death penalty in this country it's mostly the poor, mostly people of colour. The injustices involved in policing and imprisonment in this country at present are overwhelming and they are devastating families and communities of colour.

This issue even spreads beyond the issue of incarceration. I think our society in the United States is becoming increasingly punitive in many arenas of life. What's more, we are becoming more comfortable with the fact that those who are receiving punishments are disproportionately children and disproportionately marginalised people. As therapists I believe we have to initiate a dialogue about punishment and about prisons. We have to put these issues on our agenda. I don't even think they are on the agenda of most therapists at the moment.

I know that in the past you have said that one way of looking at family therapy is to see it as a response to human suffering, can you say more about this?

Even if I believe my job was limited to helping families deal with their distress, there's something about poverty and racism that's very distressing and that infiltrates every aspect of life. I can't see the world in a fragmented way. I'm not just saying that – I honestly can't, for the life of me. I keep saying to the students that I'm training that what I'm attempting to do is to help trainees become relationship experts. What

I believe we should be concerning ourselves with is trying to address human suffering in whatever manifestation it takes place. So whether it's dealing with heterosexual married couples who love each other but can't find a way to be with each other, or whether it's dealing with the First Nations people and their efforts to convince white European Americans of the ways in which they have been oppressed, I believe we need to be learning how to heal strained relationships. We need to be determined in our efforts to find ways to help people come together. I know this may sound grandiose but that's what I believe. We cannot afford to turn our eyes away from any form of suffering whether it affects us directly or not. We must find ways to play our part in responding. This, to me, is the role of the therapist.

7

Glimpses of history
and current concerns

an interview with

Olga Silverstein, Margaret Newmark
and Chris Beels

Olga Silverstein is one of the founding members of family therapy. Since 1972 she has worked as a therapist, for 25 years she was a Senior Faculty member at the Ackerman Institute for Family Therapy, and is now in private practice in New York City. Margaret Newmark is a family therapist in private practice in New York City. She has a special interest in helping people and families manage persistent mental illness. Christian Beels is a psychiatrist in private practice in New York City. He is on the faculty of the Ackerman Institute for Family Therapy. The following interview took place in New York City at the apartment of Olga Silverstein and Fred Silverstein.

I'd be very interested to hear your thoughts about the historical context of what some have called 'the family therapy movement'. Can I ask you to speak a little about what you were each doing when you first became engaged with family therapy?

Olga: Thirty-five years ago Chris and I were both working at Bronx State Hospital where issues of community mental health were a primary focus. A lot of the interest was coming from work in England where the ideas of community mental health were just beginning to be explored.

What was meant by the word 'community' at this point?

Chris: One of the ideas we were influenced by from the work in England was the thought of dividing a geographic community into areas for which a certain psychiatric facility would be responsible. The Bronx Municipal Hospital Center became seen to be responsible for the mental health of the population of the Northeast Bronx. We came to see ourselves as responsible for a certain population and we believed we needed to provide whatever care was required by the people in that area. This was a very new idea at the time. It contributed to the shape of the services because if you felt responsible for all the people who had any trouble in your area, then you started to think about who they were and what resources were available to them. These ideas of community mental health were a part of the climate of the time. When we started the Family Service of Bronx State Hospital, we were looking for a more efficient way to do community psychiatry.

Olga: These ideas pre-empted the emptying out of the large psychiatric hospitals with the idea that these people could be cared for within the community and by means other than large-scale institutions. But Chris, did this notion of community mental health pre-date family therapy?

Chris: I think they came along at about the same time, in the 1950s. There is a story about Dr John Bell who was from Massachusetts, who had been studying at the Tavistock Clinic in London in 1951. While Bell was in London, he spoke with Sutherland who told him about the work that Bowlby had been doing at their clinic which involved having the whole family of the patient come in. When Bell returned to the US he was determined to emulate the work of Bowlby and began to see whole families together. It was sometime later that Bell discovered he'd misunderstood Sutherland! Bowlby was seeing all the family members individually with an occasional conference with the whole family. But the idea of working with whole families had by this time begun!

There were, I think, a number of different sources of what has come to be known as family therapy. One involved the concern with serious mental illness and schizophrenia, but the other was the concern with children. Since the 1920s there were many institutions in the US who were concerned about children and particularly what was called juvenile delinquency. Social workers were already seeing families around these kinds of problems.

Olga: It wasn't called family therapy though.

Chris: No, it was called social work, and there weren't really theories that explained how conversations with families could be facilitated. Gradually, the discipline of family therapy was created.

Olga: That's because a range of psychiatrists began to develop theoretical understandings to explain what was happening with families and ways of intervening. Almost all the early theoreticians were male psychiatrists.

Margaret: Except for Virginia Satir who wrote 'Conjoint Family Therapy' in 1964, which was very influential.

Olga: Yes, and Lynn Hoffman also played a key role during this early period as a writer – working with practitioners to put their ideas into print.

So where were you all at this point, in your work and lives?

Olga: I was a social work aide at Bronx State Hospital in 1970. From there I went to social work school and became a social worker. I had my field placement at the Ackerman Institute and that's where I stayed for the next thirty years!

Margaret: I guess I was something that is no longer possible under insurance laws. I was raising two small children and working as a volunteer. I had heard Murray Bowen and Gregory Bateson at a conference in Boston, and I thought to myself, 'Ah! The possibility of an ethical therapy!' From there I decided to volunteer on a crisis intervention team at Bronx State Hospital where Chris was the founder and head of the Family Service. Half of those crisis teams were made up of volunteers like me.

Margaret, you mentioned that what drew you to these ideas was the possibility of an 'ethical therapy'. What were the things that people were excited about at that time?

Margaret: Actually I don't think others were talking or thinking about ethics of therapy at that time. But what caught my attention was Murray Bowen's respectful, even-handed way in which he spoke to people. He was slow and he wasn't handing out dicta. There was room for each person's way of doing things. And these things appealed to me.

Olga: That was particularly true for Murray's style, but not so for other practitioners at the time. What was intriguing for me, and for a lot of people was, that maybe, just maybe understanding context might help us to understand the individual. This was an antidote to the Freudian notions of needing to delve into the individual neurosis. Perhaps instead we could look in a different direction. We could broaden out our approach and look at the context of people's lives. That was a new idea. It wasn't just one person who was at fault. We didn't have to find a scapegoat. Instead we could look at the broader context.

Chris: This was very influenced by the work of Gregory Bateson, who was not a therapist but an anthropologist and philosopher. He was very interested in family dynamics and with Margaret Mead (they were husband and wife) had studied the kinship structures of peoples in Bali and in New Guinea. With others, Bateson developed modern systems theory and cybernetics. These were theories that recognised how many different phenomena, both biological and non-biological, share the attributes of a system. A system was seen as a unified whole consisting of interrelated parts. The system was identified as being different from the sum of its parts, and any change in one part was seen to affect the rest of the system.

How did this work inform the work of therapists?

Olga: This interest in broader systems and people's inter-relatedness informed every theoretical model. Whether it was Bowen, Ackerman or Satir, everyone was involved in the exploration of what these metaphors meant for therapy.

Chris: Put simply, people were very interested in the idea that we might find ways of changing the system that would evoke change for the individual. It was new to think that if we looked at the context of people's lives we might find ways forward that did not necessarily involve medical or psychiatric theories. A lot of the initial explorations were somewhat anti-psychiatric.

So once these explorations of context began, what were some of the directions that were taken?

Olga: A number of theoretical models were then developed. One from Palo Alto where Bateson worked with Haley, Weakland, Jackson and Satir. Another was developed by Bowen, another by Ackerman, another by Salvador Minuchin, and later the Milan team contributed a great deal. There were many different refinements of these practice models.

Chris: It was a time of rival schools if you like. And all these schools were in some way informed by Bateson's ideas.

Olga: Yes, and after Bateson died it was possible for each school to claim him as an influence!

Chris: Before he died, however, Bateson made it clear that he was truly appalled by some of the things that were done in his name by family therapists! In all of these early models of family therapy the therapist was seen as the arbiter of which story would be presented in therapy, and was the definer of what was occurring in the family.

Margaret: So when did feminism begin to influence this picture?

Olga: Feminism's influence has been relatively recent. The first paper challenging family therapy about issues of gender was written by Rachel Hare-Mustin and published in Family Process in 1978. But the push to address clinical issues from a feminist perspective really came from the Women's Project.

Could you talk a little bit about the Women's Project?

Olga: As with all ideas, the idea for the Women's Project came from various directions simultaneously. I don't think we invented it, it just happened that we came together. Marianne Walters was working in Philadelphia with Salvador Minuchin when she invited Peggy Papp, Betty Carter and me to come and present a small workshop looking at women's issues. This workshop went so well, and we enjoyed it so much, that we decided that we would present at a conference in New York. We weren't on the program for this conference so we just put a sign in the hall saying 'After lunch – women who are interested can come to such-and-such a room and chat about women's issues'. We came back from lunch late thinking that no-one would come. But when we got to the room we found 500 people in the room! We knew that the time had come.

We then held a series of open seminars, starting in New York. We divided the seminars into categories: women as mothers, women as wives, women as mothers of sons, and women as mothers of daughters. Because there were four of us – four pushy dames! – we thought it would be wise to divide the territory! Unless we knew what each of us were doing, we would all talk at once!

We found a way to work together which we enjoyed very much. Then somehow we decided we would write a book which evolved into 'The Invisible Web: Gender patterns in family relationships'. We wrote it in 1981 and it is still selling. We continued giving some workshops and then gradually it wasn't needed anymore. The ideas spread into the field and became general knowledge. I moved into a different direction, to explore the effects of the women's movement on men in families. How we raise our sons became my major feminist interest.

Whereas others, including Chris, moved in a very different direction – in seeking approaches to respond to the seriously mentally ill. I think there was a distinct division made between ways of dealing with families who were experiencing 'normal crises' and those families who were struggling with the effects of serious mental illness. It was seen that these required different methodologies.

Chris: Yes, as I mentioned earlier, concerns with schizophrenia and serious mental health issues, along with work with children, provided some of the initial energy that launched family therapy as a discipline. Many different people were involved in trying to find ways of addressing serious mental illness. Various early theories tried to explain how families cause or help to cause members to be schizophrenic. But none of these theories contributed to ideas as to how to work with families. The approaches these theories seemed to imply – of quarantining the noxious family from the patient, or performing some sort of sanitising 'therapy' on family members – far from working, often contributed to increasing the sense of guilt of family members and made it difficult or impossible for therapists to form the basis of a therapeutic relationship with the family.

Gradually alternative ways of understanding schizophrenia were developed which led to different ways of addressing it through family therapy. What's more, experimental outcome data was used to substantiate a particular form of therapy. Various researchers showed that the psycho-educational form of family therapy turned out to be more effective by far than any other sort of treatment for a particular group of people. Many other groups then began using this model. It showed that if you could demonstrate a particular approach really worked then people would learn how to do it. I think it's important to recognise that since then family therapy has been an evidence-based and empirical line of work.

Margaret: We have also found that therapists who are working in institutions or with people with serious mental illness are in need of kind supervision that is sympathetic and actively helpful. To do that work on a daily basis requires this support. Ongoing supportive conversations are very important.

What are some of the contemporary issues that family therapy is facing now?

Margaret: On the positive side, there is now a great interest in how families define their own problems. This was not true at the beginning of family therapy. Where once therapists felt at ease in defining the experiences and problems that families were facing, this is now not so true, and I believe this is a very good thing. On the downside, in the United States, managed care is probably the greatest challenge to family therapy. It is really threatening to reduce practitioner's creativity.

Olga: I am also concerned about the development of specialisation because with that narrower focus comes a narrowing of the ways of understanding families themselves. If a family goes to consult an 'incest specialist' then they become seen as an 'incest family'. If someone is consulting an 'addiction specialist' then they become to some extent defined by their problem in ways that doesn't occur in generalist practice. I believe we must prepare workers to be able to address a broad range of experiences that families face and experience. Otherwise we will be replicating certain ideas about families. Families change over time as they have to deal with different issues over time. Rather than defining a family by the particular issue they are facing at one time, I believe students have to learn to look at human beings as people who face and struggle with a range of issues over life.

Chris: At the same time, however, one of the ways in which family therapy theory has grown historically has been through groups concentrating on specific clinical problems. People have become interested in a particular kind of clinical problem and on figuring out what to do on that particular issue. The papers that are then written from these projects generate a lot of interest. What we then have to do is find a way to put these ideas into general practice.

Olga: The other big change is that first the focus of therapists was on the individual and then it moved to be on the family. Now the emphasis has moved towards the larger culture – towards ethnicity and the culture as a whole. Family therapists are much more interested now in how specific cultural and sociological problems impact on families. This is the area in which much interesting work is now taking place.

Thank you Olga, Margaret and Chris. Although I'd love to ask you all more questions, it is getting late and I know that we should wind this up. Thanks.

8

Women's stories

an interview with

Joan Laird

Joan Laird is an eminent scholar and family therapist who has made diverse contributions to the field of family therapy through her writings and teachings. Amongst other topics, some of her most influential work has concentrated on women's stories, the social construction of gender, culture and sexuality and implications for therapists. She has recently edited the book 'Lesbians and Lesbian Families: Reflections on theory and practice', and co-edited, 'Lesbians and Gays in Couples and Families: A handbook for therapists'. This interview took place in Boston, Massachusetts.

It would be great to hear about how you came to be interested in exploring women's stories and why, over many years, you've felt that this is an important realm for family therapists.

My interest in story probably began through engaging with family of origin work, as that was the first model of family therapy I became interested in. In my early work, I began to believe that families were like small societies and that they seemed to construct powerful intergenerational cultures, replete with their particular myths, stories, and rituals. It seemed to me that each family developed its own storyline or narrative, although I would not have described it in this way then. Each family had its own unique but always changing culture, and yet it wasn't just a matter of ethnicity or social traditions, it was also about that individual family's shared history and experiences. From early on, although I used them in my work, I was uneasy about structural and systemic metaphors, which seemed too mechanistic and too removed from everyday human experience.

Then, when I was teaching social work in Michigan and practicing family therapy in the late 1970s, I decided to begin doctoral study. In Ann Arbor, the social work doctorate was always a combination of social work and social science. At first, I looked to social work and psychology, and then to social work and sociology, but the family was not a topic of interest in either of these disciplines at that time. There were virtually no courses that related to the family and a quantitative research protocol, never of interest to me, dominated doctoral study in those fields. Somehow, although I had never had even an undergraduate course in anthropology, I thought perhaps that was a field whose dominant metaphor of 'culture' might fit with family study. And so I was drawn towards anthropology and became the first student enrolled in a joint social work and anthropology program.

It took me a year or two to find my way into the language of anthropology and to gain some ideas about how I might transfer categories useful in studying so-called 'traditional', 'primitive', or 'exotic' societies to the study and helping of American families. Gradually I became increasingly interested first in ritual, then in story and myth, and a few years later in narrative theory. As my experience in both anthropology and family therapy continued, I began to feel that the concepts I was learning about in anthropology were being used in the family therapy field in misguided ways. At this point, in the early 1980s, within the field of family therapy, ritual, myth, and story were referred to primarily as rigid destructive categories in family life. Most of the writing was about the damages wrought to individuals in rigidly ritualised families. These were families who had supposedly grabbed onto one story that was destructive to them. In these situations the response of the therapist was supposed to be to disabuse the family of these negative rituals, myths and stories through structural or systemic strategies. I began to believe that we as therapists were treading in areas that we knew very little about, casting a largely negative light on universal cultural family processes. We were unfamiliar with the positive, healing aspects of myth, ritual, story, and secrets – modes used in every society and in every family, for better or worse. These everyday aspects of life experience were seen not only as destructive but as 'unscientific'. There was little room for respecting or understanding such things as belief, family folklore, or spirituality in the helping professions.

In the early 1980s, immersed in reading Geertz, Turner, Myerhoff and other anthropologists digging into the meanings of ritual and story, I began to believe that story, myth, and ritual not only were terribly important in our lives, but that, actually, perhaps that was all there was. Perhaps science itself was an elaborate story, built on a mathematical metaphor. I began to understand that myth, ritual, and story were not necessarily negative or whimsical, but in fact were central categories in every culture and every family. I believed that we needed to know a lot more about them, what healthy as well as problematic purposes they might serve.

In thinking about stories, rituals, narratives, and local knowledges, I began mining for these cultural experiences from friends, in workshops, in my own family, and with the families who came for therapy. We began to see how some family stories seemed defeating and hopeless, while others seemed wonderfully connecting and healing. We started wondering how it is, from the many possibilities, that families choose particular stories, rituals, and so on to be passed down, repeated, and altered over the generations. We worked with people alone and in groups, encouraging them to make visible their family cultural symbols, metaphors, stories, and so on and to reflect on their meanings and their effects.

This was a very interesting process and I began to present and write about the significance of stories to family therapy. But I had some difficulty getting these findings published. Although I did publish a paper on ritual in 1983, in general the social work journals felt my writings were 'unscientific'. It wasn't until Monica McGoldrick, Carol Anderson and Froma Walsh organised the Stonehenge women's conferences that I was offered another outlet for my work. The Stonehenge conferences opened up opportunities for everyone who participated. In preparing for my presentation there, I began to think more in particular about how women's lives were being storied, and how women's stories were suppressed and trivialised in various ways. Following this presentation, Monica, Froma, and Carol invited me to write a paper for their book titled 'Women in Families'. It was in that book, in 1989, that I finally was able to publish a paper about the stories of women's lives and their relevance to family therapy. About the same time, Evan Imber-Black, Janine Roberts, and Richard Whiting asked me to do a chapter on ritual for their book 'Rituals in Families and in Family Therapy.'

The chapter, 'Women and stories: Restorying women's self-constructions' is a beautiful paper. Within it, you describe some of the different sorts of stories that are available to men that aren't available to women, and also some gendered differences in relation to genres of speech. Can you say something about these explorations and what they mean in terms of therapy?

Some of what I wrote derived from my own experiences in the family therapy field and from endless discussions with other women about the silencing and discounting of our voices. To a large extent, public discourse remained the province of men. I remember my first university-wide faculty meetings, and my first appointment to a university committee and realising that I didn't understand the language that was being spoken. I didn't understand the rules of the discourse, who could speak, and how speeches were to be made. These were not speech genres that I as a woman had been schooled in. I began to read the literature on conversation, narrative, and discourse, and to observe my own world in new ways. What I learned was that there are particular areas of talk and ways of talking that are largely reserved for men and others that are reserved for women. Women's talk is generally constructed as domestic, as private. It is often characterised as gossipy, frivolous, and trivial. It is undervalued and restricted far more to private than public spaces. Although that is still largely the case, I think that more and more women have been learning to talk in public spaces and are claiming the podium. To what extent women have created their own ways of speaking in public, or have simply adopted the public speech patterns used by men, is another whole realm of study, which hasn't been my particular area of interest.

In terms of what these explorations mean for therapy, one of the implications is for therapists to observe the ways in which everyday narratives are gendered. In my work I began to question more consciously how people had absorbed the larger gender stories in their cultural surrounds, and how these gendered stories were positively affecting or constraining their lives and their relationships. I also began asking people to think about these gendered stories, where they had come from, and whether they were working well for them in the present.

Generally speaking though, I was far more interested in theory than I was in the actual practices of therapy. One of the many things that was inspiring about 'Narrative Means to Therapeutic Ends', by Michael White and David Epston, was that they were drawing upon some of the same anthropological work that I had been reading – Barbara Myerhoff, Victor Turner, Clifford Geertz, Michel Foucault – but they had gone on to develop creative ways of integrating many of the ideas into their therapeutic practice. Their work was fascinating to me at the time and continues to be, not only their focus on narrative but also on power and the politics of practice.

Can I ask you about some of the broader themes that you and other women in family therapy at the Stonehenge gatherings were exploring in relation to re-storying women's lives?

At the first women's conference, Ann Hartman and I co-led an evening workshop on 'women and story' in which we looked at women's myths and family therapy. One of the questions we wished to explore was, 'Who was in charge of writing the family therapy story in general and women's participation in particular? How was the *his*tory of family therapy being produced?' We had a clear sense that women were being either written out or their contributions minimised in this history-making process. We decided that the one person in family therapy who might be labelled a heroine, or mythical figure, was Virginia Satir. I wasn't a particular follower of Satir's work but I had experienced on a number of occasions hearing leading male family therapists make very disparaging or trivialising remarks about her. Part of my interest in looking at how the myth of Virginia Satir was being constructed came from my experience in examining the ways in which Margaret Mead's work and she herself were being ridiculed in some of my male taught anthropology classes and in publishing. The history of anthropological study was largely a history of males studying males, yet this woman had made the terrible mistake of becoming the best known anthropologist in the world. She had to be cut down to size, and I suspected the same might be true of Satir. Mead was being portrayed as not only a poor scientist and a poor mother, but also as masculine and, when all else failed, probably a lesbian. I wondered if the same might be the case with Satir, probably the most famous family therapist of her time.

At our workshop, women began telling stories about Satir. At first these stories all were disparaging, until one person spoke out in relation to a widely told story and said, 'You know that story you just told … I was there when that incident happened, and it did not happen as you described. This is what happened'. From that point on, the discussion became very animated and politicised. As women, we started asking each other from whom we had heard various versions of this particular story. There was a common thread regarding its source. Over time, we began to understand that the control over the stories of Satir's life and work, indeed of women's contributions in the family therapy field, were not in women's hands. Some of the women began to tell other stories about Satir, positive stories, heroic stories. It was really an exercise in beginning to take charge of our own history as women in the field. The Stonehenge conferences were held at a time when women were struggling to find their places in the family field. Those conferences played a powerful role in jumpstarting that process.

It would be great to hear also about the history of family therapy in relating to gay and lesbian lives. I know that you have played a significant part in speaking and writing about these issues …

I certainly don't see myself as a pioneer in this area. Ann (Hartman) and I have been part of the family therapy movement since its early years, and I'm sure everyone in the family therapy field who knew us, knew that we were a couple. But this was never openly articulated, either by us or by anyone else, outside of our lesbian friendship network, until the early 1990s. Throughout the 1960s and 1970s, even in my home situation, I was living a closeted life. Even my son didn't have a language to describe or explain my relationship with Ann, though she had come into our lives when he was just sixteen months old. I was just as homophobic as almost everyone else in the family therapy movement, except that I was terrified too, and with good reason, both personally and professionally. Most of all I feared losing custody of my son, a real threat during his growing up years. Throughout the 1980s, I was certainly very admiring of my students and my clients who were out, and I greatly admired Claudia Bepko, JoAnn Krestan, and Sallyann Roth, who were speaking and publishing on lesbian lives in the family therapy field.

In the early 1990s, Sallyann pointed out to me that, at that point, she was the only person writing about lesbian issues in family therapy. She had become the token 'expert' on this topic in the family field and was being asked to do just about everything that came up. She told me that when one was willing to present and publish on lesbian themes, one quickly became a 'professional lesbian', a master status that could quickly make invisible other aspects of one's work. In the early 1990s, when Sallyann was asked to do a plenary at AFTA, this time by Froma Walsh, she declined and directed Froma to me, thereby pushing me into a personal crisis. After having a major anxiety attack, and taking a week to decide, I accepted the invitation and participated in a gay and lesbian plenary alongside Gary Sanders and John Patten. At about the same time, Froma also asked me to write a chapter on gay and lesbian families for the second edition of her book 'Normal Family Processes'. Coming out professionally in this way began a major re-storying of my own life. Although at first it was very anxious making for me, I began to introduce a new language, the language of lesbianism, into my public and professional life. In exploring the literature, the research, and becoming more exposed to lesbian culture, I was startled to learn how much this study opened new windows into mainstream culture, much like anthropological study of another culture helps us better understand our own. I've been writing about lesbian and gay people's lives and relationships ever since, master status or not, and I am grateful to Froma and to Sallyann for opening that door and gently pushing me through it.

One of the questions that the field of family therapy has had to engage with due to feminism and lesbian and gay perspectives, has been, 'What is a family?' Can you say a little about this?

There has always been an irony in relation to feminism and family therapy. In the early days of the second wave of feminism, the family was seen as the site of the greatest oppression of women. Lesbian feminists for the most part were very definitely anti-family. Before the 1980s most lesbian-headed families consisted of a parent who had had children in the context of a heterosexual marriage or relationship. It wasn't until the 1980s that what was to become known as the 'lesbian baby boom' began to take hold, that is, single and coupled lesbians becoming pregnant through donor insemination. During the same period, an increasing number of lesbians sought to adopt children. These shifts, the AIDS crisis, and a growing culture of acceptance, led more and more gay and lesbian couples to began to actively define themselves as family. Part of this involved claiming rights to children, but some of it was also about claiming rights to family definition. The most recent evidence of gay men and lesbians wanting to be defined as 'families' can be seen in the same-sex marriage movement in many countries throughout the world. We are, in fact, engaged in cultural wars over the definition of 'family'.

More recently, historian Lillian Faderman and others have traced a long history of relationships and families in which women were living together in couples, or in committed relationships with other women. Before the twentieth century, these women did not call themselves lesbian, because at the time there was no such social category, but in tracing this history Faderman has demonstrated that these families have always existed. I don't think we spring from ashes with no past to follow.

Feminist family therapists, both heterosexual and lesbian, continue to question and challenge many of the family therapy field's normative theoretical assumptions about family life. Questions such as 'what constitutes a family', and 'what are family values' are being hotly debated in this country still. These days, here in the States, gay and lesbian people are claiming the right to civil unions and to the legal right to marry. The field of family therapy has had to change to keep up with the changing values of the culture, and this process will need to continue.

Speaking of ongoing challenges to the field, I know that recently you have been thinking and writing around transgender issues and what they might mean for family therapy. Can you say a little about this?

My students have been my best teachers. For several years before I retired from teaching, I taught, among other things, a gender and sexuality course about and for women, and a lesbian identity course. In these and other courses, I did my best to include discussions around transgender and transsexual experiences, finding the students more fascinated with these issues than any other. Recently, I've had the good fortune to come to know some transsexual and transgender persons and to learn from them. In reading the literature, observing popular culture and, in general, engaging more with this issue, I've become more aware of the contributions that transgender people and transsexual people are making to our society. It seems to me that, more than anyone else, they are helping to alter the entire social discourse on how we think about gender, how we think about sexuality, and the ways in which gender and sexuality are constructed and connected.

When thinking about transgender and transsexual experience, there are so many questions to consider in terms of changing social definition and social place. I have also become intrigued about the experience of partners of people who undergo transition. What would it mean for you if your partner changed gender? And what does such a transition mean in terms of relationships with extended families and others? These are some of the questions I am very engaged with just now. There is always so much to think through! The field of family therapy is about engaging with the rituals, myths, and stories of people's lives. To me, that makes the field quite remarkable. I hope we remain open to all of the contradictions and complexities of people's stories. That's what keeps a field creative and relevant.

9

Reflecting family therapy

an interview with

Tom Andersen

Tom Andersen, from Tromsø, Norway, is an influential figure within the field of family therapy. He is credited with, amongst other things, having revolutionised the use of reflecting teams in therapy. The following interview took place in Oslo at the Family Therapy World Congress.

It would be great to hear your views on how family therapy has evolved here in Norway, and some of the specific contributions that Norwegian family therapy have made to the broader field ...

Norwegian family therapists have been very influenced by work from other countries, especially the work of Harry Goolishian and Harlene Anderson as well as by the Milan team. The work of Michael White and David Epston is also very popular here, as is Steve de Shazer's work. The reflecting processes that we have developed in the north of Norway have also been influential. There are many different kinds of reflecting processes that are now being experimented with and applied.

If I was to concentrate on a single influence on my work, it would be that of Harry Goolishian who was a good friend to Norway. Many people here loved him dearly. He helped us to be friendly and generous in terms of time and attention. He was also wonderful at connecting with people. He never connected with a person's insufficiencies but only with the parts of the person which are good, the parts of the person which wanted something different, to do no harm. His concept of language systems, systems that are created through the ways people speak to each other around the problem, has been very helpful. He spoke about problem-creating language systems and problem-dissoluting language systems, and these have been valuable thinking tools.

I have tried to take Harry's ideas forward by defining language as all the expressions we give. Language is more than words, it includes all the activities of the body. This emphasis has derived from my work with physiotherapists over the last thirty years. The movements of our bodies, dance, painting, the arts, rhythm and music are all aspects of our expressions of life and I have been very interested in how these can contribute to the field of family therapy. I have been focusing on body work and am interested in expanding the repertoire of what we consider as expressions of our selves. I am not so interested in the end product of our expressions – the creation of a new story for example, or finding a solution. Instead, my interest is simply in enabling people to widen the repertoire of their expressions and this often in itself takes care of the problem.

When a physiotherapist helps someone to stretch the body and open up their front side and release their breathing, the words and stories come by themselves. Physiotherapists do not search for the story behind the tense body, they just work with the body to help people to loosen up the movements, to stretch. This stretching creates new possibilities by itself. I think this metaphor has much to offer the field of family therapy.

There have been a number of ways in which your thinking has stretched the field! Can you speak a little about the reflecting processes you have developed?

I like to take a broader view on reflecting processes by referring to the work of the French philosopher Imanuel Levinos, who died about four or five years ago. He wrote about the differences between a philosophy of ethics and a philosophy of ontology. Ontology is the science of explaining what something is. It asks the questions, what is a human being? what is a problem? what is a good outcome? It involves explaining or understanding something through observation, through being an observer. A philosophy of ethics, on the other hand, pays attention to what goes on between people when we are together. It involves trying to find a way to work together through which the dignity of both parties is protected, and nobody is hurt or humiliated. I believe in prioritising a philosophy of ethics, and asking the question, what am I responsible for in relation to my interactions with others?

Some people engage with reflecting processes by becoming observers and they make some kind of judgement about the family – this is a nice family, this is a struggling family, this is a dysfunctional family. Then they start to instruct the family, even if this occurs in a very nice way. To observe, define and instruct is to prioritise a philosophy of ontology. This is one way of engaging with reflecting team processes and I regret these ways badly. This was the way family therapy reflecting processes used to be done, and still are done in some circumstances.

Another way of engaging with reflecting processes is to concentrate on the relationships and to give back in the reflections how the family's story has influenced the person who has heard it. Now we do not try to analyse the stories that we hear. We instead speak about what it means to hear the stories and what it has led us to start thinking about. For example, 'When I heard the father say this or that, I became a bit sad and my thoughts started to concentrate on the question of who could the father speak with about this? I began to wonder whether it is possible to find someone who is willing to understand the father? And who should that be? How could the father present his dilemma to them?' The person reflecting is saying something about the effect of hearing the story upon themselves and then asking some questions which are offered in a spirit which honours the relationship.

This is what we are trying to do in the north of Norway, but there are still many observers and instructors, even in our community. We are trying to avoid being instructors and observers and to concentrate on a philosophy of ethics rather than a philosophy of ontology.

Would you like to speak about some of the ways in which people have taken up these ideas about reflecting processes?

Many people have liked these ideas for different reasons. This sort of reflecting talk investigates a certain issue from many different perspectives – what does the mother think of it? what does the father think of it? what does the doctor think of it? what does the person at the bank think about it? We let people speak freely which we think is very important. We are interested in creating meetings in which every person can have their voice heard without being interrupted. And each person then hears back from the team what the team members have heard. The process of the family first talking and then the team commenting has impacted on the ways in which the team listens. This is perhaps the most important effect of these ways of working.

Listening has been very undervalued in western society. To be a speaker is very respected, but we are trying to not speak so much but instead to listen. Harry Goolishian always said we needed to 'listen to what people really say and not to what they really mean'. He believed that when we listen to what people really mean we are actually interpreting what they are saying from our own perspective. We have tried simply to listen to what people say.

Having the team of therapists speak openly in front of the family was also a new development wasn't it? Prior to this, reflecting teams were generally anonymous weren't they? Not only were they instructing families, but they were sometimes behind the screen without ever meeting the family members ...

Yes. I regret these past practices very much. We were originally fearful of what we might say if we spoke in front of the family. We were concerned we would not be respectful, as team members were not respectful when the team was anonymous behind the screen. But we found that changing the structure itself changed the ways in which we spoke, and the ways in which we listened.

We now have a network of people from Denmark, Norway, Sweden, Finland, Northwest Russia, Estonia, Lithuania, and Latvia who have all been meeting together over the last five years. There are thirty groups in these different countries working with reflecting processes in response to psychotic crises. We are using reflecting processes where once we would have used neuroleptic medication and hospitalisation. We have been having quite some success. The network is our meeting place for exchanging ideas. We are learning from each other. We have practical discussions as well as philosophical discussions about what we believe about psychotic crises. In some respects we feel that psychotic crises are times in which people have no words to describe the difficult situations they are experiencing.

You said earlier that your aim in therapeutic work is to broaden the repertoire of self-expression. Does this ideal also fit with the reflecting processes – that their aim is to create more possibilities of expression, for people to hear a diversity of expressions from others so that conversations that otherwise would not occur can take place?

Very much so. Our ambitions are small. The conversations are not goal orientated or product orientated, but are based entirely around the process.

What do you see as some of the challenges facing the field of family therapy at the moment?

My greatest concern is that the market economy is so strong that it encourages techniques and what brings money quickly. I am concerned that therapy might become more orientated towards the needs of the therapist and less and less for the people. My concern is that a philosophy of ontology will be placed above a philosophy of ethics. Very many in the field are occupied with learning techniques in ways that are dehumanising. I am worried that the language of technology and the language of money are beginning to preoccupy therapists, encouraging them to become effective observers and fixers.

There are hopeful developments happening also. Here in Norway, psychiatric patients are beginning to present in conferences where they tell the stories of what was helpful and what was not helpful in relation to professional interactions. There are many exciting developments like this occurring as well as changes that are gradually taking place within organisations and even bureaucracies within which we are working. Recently I have been involved in working within bureaucratic cultures – trying to change meetings away from consisting of instructing others to discussions involving questions and reflecting processes. The changes that are taking place are amazing and I have changed my prejudice towards bureaucrats totally!

I strongly believe that all therapists who are committed to examining the politics of therapy must remain companions in encouraging the field to let a philosophy of ethics come before a philosophy of ontology. There are many differences in ideas in the field of family therapy – many profound differences in basic assumptions – and this I believe is a good thing, yet there is also much in common. We must remain engaged in these broader struggles together.

10

The process of
changing family therapy

an interview with

Peggy Papp

Peggy Papp is a senior supervisor and Director of the Depression Program at the Ackerman Institute; the Director of Family Therapy at North General Hospital, Dept. of Psychiatry; author of 'The Process of Change', co-author of 'The Invisible Web', and editor of 'Couples on the Fault Line'. Peggy has received lifetime achievement awards from The American Family Therapy Academy and The American Association for Marriage and Family Therapy. Peggy maintains a private practice in New York City where this interview took place. Cheryl White and David Denborough were present. David was the interviewer.

Peggy, you have made so many different contributions to the field, it is difficult to know where to begin. Can I ask you perhaps how you first became interested in family therapy?

Well my first career was as an actress. And so when I applied to a school of social work I was turned down because I had been in the theatre and they thought I wouldn't be serious about my work. They told me I first had to get a job and prove I was really committed to following through. But how could I get a job without a degree? There was only one place I could work without a degree and that was the Bureau of Child Welfare. So that's where I went. After working there for a year I returned to the School of Social Work and they accepted me.

As it turned out, the job at the Bureau of Child Welfare proved to be serendipitous because while I was there they showed a training film in which Nathan Ackerman was working with a family. I didn't know what he did nor how he did it, I only knew it was powerful. He changed the ways in which family members were reacting and responding to each other. And I said to myself then and there, 'this is what I want to do'. But when I graduated from Social Work School there were no family therapy institutes. So I got a very conventional job in a child psychiatry department. Only the psychiatrists were allowed to treat the children who were considered to be very fragile and precious. The social workers could see the families I guess because they thought the families were really beyond repair and it wouldn't matter what damage we social workers did to them!

I remember a particular case in which a child psychiatrist was working with a child and wasn't getting anywhere, and I was working with the child's family and wasn't getting anywhere, and so I summoned up my courage and said, 'Listen, how would you like to do a little subversive therapy, you know, go underground and have a family therapy session?' And he said 'Why not'. So we actually snuck in and out of the room with the family. This sounds ludicrous now because the family lived together, but to have a therapy session with them all in the same room was actually unheard of at the time.

Once we had the family all together in the room though, we realised that we didn't know what to do! So I went to the phone and called Nathan Ackerman. I had heard he had started some kind of an institute by then. I told him I wanted to learn to do family therapy and he made an appointment to see me.

I will never forget my first interview with him. He was a very unconventional man. I was so nervous and I had prepared a curriculum vitae with all of my credentials. I took these and laid them reverentially on his desk. Ackerman looked at them and said 'What the hell are those?' I said 'They're my credentials'. He promptly threw them off the desk into the wastepaper basket, leaned over and said 'Do you have a heart?' I said tremulously, 'Yes, it's in my throat right now, but I have a heart, yes'. He said, 'We want somebody with a heart – are you the person for the job?' I said 'Yes, yes, I'm the person'. Anyway, I got the job. I was the first social worker hired at the Ackerman Institute. So, that's the way I got started in family therapy!

What an extraordinary story! What was it like working at the Ackerman in those early days?

It was very exciting. I felt I was on the cutting edge of a revolutionary movement. Ackerman was giving live family demonstrations at psychiatric conferences which sent shock waves through the whole psychiatric profession. New ideas were popping up all around – from Murray Bowen, Salvador Minuchin, Jay Haley, Paul Watzlawick – so many fascinating ideas and possibilities.

But although Ackerman was a great innovator, he was not a good teacher. He used to supervise me by calling me out from behind the one-way mirror and saying 'Relax, you're uptight!' For some reason this never made me relax. He knew what he knew, but it would be like Caruso trying to teach you to sing by saying 'you just open your mouth and you sing'. I learned by the seat of my pants, by watching him and reading everything I could get my hands on and then trying each new idea as they came down the pike.

After a while they asked me to teach. I didn't think I knew anything but I said to myself, 'Well, I probably know one more thing than they do.' So, I began to teach and Betty Carter and Olga Silverstein were among my first students. We still joke about those first days because I had no idea what I was doing. Then one day Betty Carter came running to me and said, 'Peggy, I just read this book by Murray Bowen. Guess what, there's a theory to family therapy!' I said, 'Really?' She said, 'Yeah, there are concepts and you can draw triangles and squares and there are building blocks, and you can put them all together'. I said 'Wow'! What do you know, a theory!'

So I read Murray Bowen, and fell in love with his ideas. With Betty Carter, Phil Geuren, and Tom Fogarty, we formed the Center for Family Learning based on Bowen's concepts. During this time I would go home and have long conversations with my family of origin. I really worked hard trying to 'differentiate' myself from my family. Some of my attempts were very funny. I remember going home once when I was trying to get 'emotionally unhooked' from certain family interactions. We were having this big picnic out in the grass and I was very proud of how well I was doing. But then my sister said something that pushed one of my sensitive buttons and I began acting like a three-year-old. My 'non-reactive' stance went out the window and I started to fight with her. My other sister got involved in it and my brother who had a video camera began to film the whole scene. We were all yelling and screaming and crying. So I decided to show the video to my trainees as an example of what not to do. The video is titled, 'Peggy Papp Differentiating Herself From Her Family of Origin'.

Was it in these early days that you first developed your work around the use of sculpture in therapy?

Yes. I first developed it in relation to Murray Bowen's family of origin ideas. I asked families to arrange themselves in a physical sculpture that reflected the way in which they experienced their various positions in the family. It was an effort to project the family system outward into a living moving picture that you could experience being part of emotionally but at the same time you could stand outside of it and look at it. My first training tape, 'Making the Invisible Visible', is based on this idea.

I then developed many different forms of sculpting. Some of these were of epic proportions such as when I did the three generation sculpting. Later on, I developed what I refer to as 'couples choreography' which I still use today. I ask couples to have a fantasy about their relationship and to imagine the symbolic forms in which they would appear in a fantasy. Then I ask them to enact their fantasies with each other. This provides a metaphorical description of the relationship rather than a literal one and the therapist can then use these unique metaphors throughout the therapy.

I stopped experimenting with the sculpting when I moved on to other ideas but every once in a while somebody will come up to me and remind me that I sculpted their family twenty years ago and they still remember how it changed their lives. When I hear this I think perhaps I should revisit that technique after all. There is something very powerful in experiencing a situation rather than just talking about it.

How did you become engaged with the ideas of paradox in therapy?

Over time, I began to feel that some of the ideas related to family of origin work were limited, that they didn't deal with what's happening in the here and now. So when Minuchin asked me to teach at the Philadelphia Child Guidance Clinic I began to watch him and Jay Haley. I had always been fascinated by the ironies, the contradictions and paradoxes of life and began experimenting with them in my work.

One day Gillian Walker came running to me and said 'Peggy, I see you're interested in paradoxical interventions. I've just read this book by Mara Selvini-Palazzoli an Italian psychiatrist. Her book's not published here but I can give it to you.' I read Mara's book and was so impressed that I immediately called her. I said, 'Hullo, I'm a social worker calling from America. I'm fascinated by your work and I want to come and see it.' The only problem was, I had forgotten about the time-change and I had called her in the middle of the night. So Mara said, 'Well, yes, come, but not in the middle of the night!'

Anyway, I travelled to Italy and observed the Milan team working. I felt I had found a vein of gold. Their ideas really turned everything on its head. And the ways in which they used rituals and ceremonies to dramatise and change relationships was very intriguing.

When I returned to the Ackerman Institute I conveyed my enthusiasm to Olga Silverstein and asked her to come with me to Milan to observe the team. She did and as a result we set up the Brief Therapy Project at the Ackerman Institute based on paradoxical ideas. But we quickly modified the ideas to suit our own style. I felt uncomfortable in giving one message to the family which only prescribed the symptom. So we began adding a contradictory message from the team which supported change – such as 'The team does not agree that Johnny needs to continue to distract his parents from their problems. They believe the parents are perfectly capable of resolving their problems without the help of Johnny.' This message prescribed change as well as homeostasis and is what I refer to in 'The Process of Change' as the 'therapeutic debate'. We sometimes added a third position which contradicted the first two. The third was usually directed towards a child such as 'It doesn't matter what anyone else in your family does, you need to do what is best for you'.

The family became the audience to their own play, listening to their family drama being debated from three different positions. They could then reflect on the different possibilities being discussed and decide for themselves which direction they wanted to go in. When we first began using this technique we got nothing short of miraculous results. We thought we'd found the magic key. Then as always, we found the magic key didn't always work.

It seems that during those earlier years you were very deliberately immersing yourself within these different ways of working, experimenting with them until you could find your own way. Can you say a little about this?

Yes, I think that is true. I know others in the field tend to stay more with one way of working. I have an urge to always be trying something new. This has its negative as well as positive sides. The negative is that when you try something new, you have to be willing to give up being an expert and go back to being a student. Which is what I did every time I changed my model. I would stumble, flounder, fall on my face, feel like an utter fool. And there would be times when I knew if I went back to using my old familiar model it would probably work but then I would never learn to do anything different. It was a matter of having the patience to teach myself a new way of thinking. And I'm glad I did. I am especially glad that I moved away from working with paradoxical interventions to a focus on belief systems and themes. These are much more effective because they take into account meanings that paradox ignores – such as gender, class, race, culture, etc.

I would like to ask you about 'The Women's Project' that you initiated with Betty Carter, Olga Silverstein and Marianne Walters. The work that you did together, and your book, 'The Invisible Web', so completely altered the ways in which the field of family therapy understood issues of gender. Can you say a little bit about this?

The reason we formed the project was because none of the systems concepts took gender differences into account. For example, the common concept of reciprocity held that everyone involved in an interaction played an equal part in the maintenance of that interaction by reinforcing the behaviour of the other. This assumed everyone shared equal power and equal responsibility which ignores gender and age differences. There is a distinction between a person being involved in an interaction and being responsible for that interaction. It's hard for me to believe now, but I myself subscribed to this concept when I was working with the cybernetic model. I can remember with a combination of shame and disbelief many years ago turning to a wife and saying, 'What do you do to provoke your husband's violence?' Although it seems shocking now, it was not a shocking question at the time.

Another concept we challenged is the concept of 'neutrality'. I think it is now accepted that there is no such thing as 'neutrality' in any interpersonal encounter. Nor should there be, especially where physical abuse is involved. Abuses of any kind require therapists to take moral and ethical positions. 'The Invisible Web' was one of the first books to give specific guidelines for translating feminist ideas into clinical practice.

In the process of writing the book we had to scrutinise our own gender beliefs and practices and this was a very enlightening experience for me because I began to realise how much my own life and relationships were dominated by my beliefs. It was this realisation that led me to begin working with belief systems in therapy.

Peggy, You've been such a significant figure within the field for many years now, it would be great to hear your reflections on where the field has come from and where it is heading now ...

I think that the technological, biological and genetic revolutions that are taking place will drastically change the way we do therapy. All of these scientific advances will not only alter our theoretical concepts but the means of practising therapy. They already have. There is a burgeoning of internet therapy which is taking many different forms – e-mail therapy, support groups of every kind and on-line training courses and lectures. All of these make therapy more available to people around the world. They also challenge one of the field's most time-honoured ideas – that physical presence is essential to the therapeutic process.

Our field has always reflected the changing values and ideas of our times. We've had to adapt our models to accommodate to each of the social and cultural changes that have taken place over the years – such as the women's movement, the sexual revolution, changing political and social values and life styles. We've had to alter our very definition of family. Which kind of family? Single parent, blended, surrogate, gay and lesbian, cross-cultural, families of choice, reconstructed? We now have multiple definitions of family each with different structures, needs, styles and resources.

In the beginning it was so simple. The focus was mainly on the nuclear family and all we had to do was change the interactional cycles and help family members to communicate better. Then we became aware of the impact of larger systems and had to expand out concepts to include those of gender, race, ethnicity and class. The debates were over which set of techniques could best accomplish this: structural, strategic, experiential, paradoxical, and more recently narrative.

In the future, debates will be over ideology rather than methodology. The new discoveries in biology and genetics are changing the very meaning of life and death. Cloning, genetically altered human beings, unprecedented life extension, and mind-controlling drugs will alter the way we think and live. We will have to face such mind-blowing questions as whether or not to tamper with 'human nature'. The questions will be: 'What is human nature and is it worth preserving? Can you genetically alter human beings to have better relationships? Will it change their need for love, togetherness, sharing, personal acknowledgement? Is it possible or desirable to erase jealousy, competition, greed, guilt, anxiety? If so, what other kinds of problems will arise?'

These are some of the awesome questions and challenges that we will face in this next century. I have this fantasy that fifty or a hundred years from now people will look back on the way we do therapy now in the same way we regard the old medical practice of bleeding people and say, 'Can you believe they used to think it was helpful to "talk about problems"!'

One thing is certain, our field can no longer remain isolated from other sciences. We must incorporate and integrate other fields of knowledge into our practices. But then who, rather than we, are more capable of doing this since the basis for our work is the systems concept that 'nothing in the universe can be understood outside its context'. I think we will have a real contribution to make.

11

Working with adversity and change

an interview with

Arnon Bentovim

Arnon Bentovim lives and works in the UK. Trained in psychiatry, psychoanalysis and family therapy, he practices as a Child and Family Psychiatrist. He is the co-author of 'Family Therapy: Complementary frameworks of theory and practice'. The following interview took place over breakfast in London.

To begin, can you say a little bit about your early contact with the ideas of family therapy?

I began my psychiatric training at the Maudsley Hospital here in London in the early 1960s when the major influences were psychoanalytic models of thinking, as well as the double-bind theory of schizophrenia. When I did my first residency in child psychiatry the tradition was that people in the family were always seen separately – the child and each parent were seen individually. At that time, in the traditional world of child psychiatry, the idea of bringing family members together into one consultation met with enormous resistance. It was felt that seeing people together could only result in 'contamination'. It wasn't until the late 1960s, early 1970s, when the family therapy movement really took off in the UK, that these ideas and many others began to be questioned and alternative models for working with families were proposed. A number of conferences were held with therapists from the Ackerman Institute from New York and various therapists such as Sal Minuchin and the Milan team began to visit London regularly. We began to work with all the family members in the room together, and we were excited and hopeful about the possibilities for meaningful change in the lives of those who were consulting us.

The early 1970s was also when the issue of child abuse began to be talked about for the first time in the health professions. I know that trying to address this issue has been a major focus of your work. Can you say a little about this?

Yes, just as I became engaged with family work, so the existence of abuse within families started to be uncovered. Early in my career I was asked to be in charge of child protection in the hospital in which I was working and so began a long involvement with families in which abuse had been disclosed. Of course, the other dynamic which became increasingly relevant through the 1980s was the feminist revolution, which began to ask questions about the power relationships within families, and began to question whether a family approach was always appropriate if the least powerful members had no voice.

These were challenging times. We had only just been developing ways of working with family groups when we had to undo the process in order to address the questions feminism was raising. We began to acknowledge that in some situations we would first need to work with individuals in order for later family work to be possible. I was soon spending half my time working with family groups, and the other half working with issues of serious abuse where families had to be separated because we couldn't work together with an abuser and a child. I currently work in a unit that specialises in working with young people who are seriously abusive, and again there we have to work separately with these young people before they can return to their families.

Looking at issues of abuse and power within families has also meant that therapists and health professionals have had their own practices questioned. I'd love to hear your thoughts about the implications this has had ...

I think that's a very interesting issue. As I just mentioned, I now work with a unit for young offenders in which the focus day-in day-out is on people's misuse of power. The young people, who are often mandated to be at this unit and who may have had lives affected by issues of race, culture and class, become very skilled at seeing how workers may at times be trying to be inappropriately powerful. These young people are acutely aware of the effects of workers' acts of domination. And so, I agree with you that working with issues of abuse means that we must become increasingly sensitive to the ways in which therapeutic practices can themselves involve the misuse of power, or be taken up into practices of control and/or domination.

In working with families these considerations are also vital. In many circumstances in which children may be taken from families due to considerations of abuse, the parents of these families are often absolutely correct in their analysis of the ways in which injustices of the society have greatly contributed to their children being removed. This is especially relevant in terms of ethnic diversity and I believe as professionals we have a lot of work to do to reduce these injustices.

Over the last fifteen years there has been a questioning of many therapeutic practices in terms of relations of power. I think it's appropriate for us to continue to ask ourselves questions about our practice as we try to generate therapeutic practices that are open and transparent. We can never deny that as therapists and health professionals we are in positions of authority. We are employed to do particular tasks. But the issue is how do we use that authority? I think that generally speaking the field of family therapy is moving towards more open and egalitarian approaches. The notion of co-constructing realities, of working alongside those that consult us, of being transparent about the thinking that informs our practice, all of these are important developments. And all of them are relatively recent in the field.

I know that you are currently in the process of organising an International Family Therapy conference which is to be held in London next year. Can you say a little bit about the sorts of themes you hope will be discussed there, and why you feel these are important at this time for the field of family therapy?

In a sense the major task that gave rise to the family therapy movement has been achieved. There's nobody that needs convincing, as they did in the early 1960s, that working with families is what's required. The question now is how can we help those many professionals who now work with families to work effectively, especially around some of the major contextual issues of our time. Recently here in the UK there has been an increasing focus on working with refugee families, managing ethnic diversity, working with families in the most disadvantaged communities, and working with trauma. I wanted to find a way of gathering these sorts of issues together and so for the International Family Therapy Association Conference (2nd-6th September 2002) we have chosen a theme of 'working with adversity and change'.

You were talking earlier about how child abuse was being uncovered at the same time as you were beginning to engage with the field of family therapy and the effects that this had upon your thinking and practice. Do you think there are similar dilemmas and challenges for the field today?

Just as we had to struggle to find a language to describe the effects that abuse has within families, I think that now we need to begin to think about how traumatic events influence whole communities and societies. I was one of the psychiatrists who was involved in interviewing the boys who were responsible for the death of James Bulger which is a case that's gone literally around the world. Although I'm not able to comment on the particularities of that case, I would like to say a few words about its broader implications. The actions of those two boys had a profound traumatic effect not only on James Bulger and his family and their friends, but also on the boys who committed the crime and their families and friends. But there was also an extraordinary effect on the broader community and indeed on the entire country.

This was a trauma that has been replayed time after time in the media – not unlike how for individuals a traumatic event may become a flashback, a memory triggered by all sorts of different situations. Every time something happens which is related to the killing of James Bulger the images are replayed on television, and there is a further outburst of distress, of sorrow, of anguish and often anger. Just as we once had to come to terms with the unspoken effects that child abuse and other forms of violence were having in our families, now I believe it is time for us to address the effects that certain traumatic events have on individuals, families and the broader community. Not only must we find ways to facilitate the healing of individuals in relation to these traumatic situations but also the broader community.

And you would see the field of family therapy as having something to offer in this realm?

Yes. One of the key skills of family therapists involves being able to speak with many different people of different ages and perspectives. Family therapists have to learn how to work with a family with a three-year-old, a ten-year-old, a sixteen-year-old, a mother, a new partner, an old partner, a grandparent etc. In other words, one of the skills we have is to work with disparate groups of people that aren't unified, and to generate a language that will unite people rather than specialise and separate. These skills can, I believe, be applied to working with community groups on these broader traumas. Our belief in connectedness, and our commitment to find ways of enabling people to talk about what was once unspeakable will also be relevant and important. I believe that family therapists have a role to play in trying to address the broader traumas that affect our communities. It will be a great challenge but it is one which I think we are ready for.

12

Talking about the future

an interview with

Elspeth McAdam

Elspeth McAdam is a highly respected child psychiatrist and systemic therapist who also works as a trainer and supervisor to health, education and social service agencies in Scandinavia, and a consultant to projects in schools in a number of European countries, Zimbabwe and Colombia. The following interview took place at the Family Therapy World Congress in Oslo, Norway, in which Elspeth McAdam and Peter Lang were presenting on 'Narratives of the future: Dreamtalk working to create hope and healing for children and their families'.

Elspeth, I was wondering whether we could begin with how you have come to be doing the sort of work you are currently involved in?

After completing my child psychiatry studies which had involved some group analytic training, I went on to become a cognitive therapist. From the beginning though I had a belief that one really needed to be concerned with the whole family, rather than simply focusing on the child. As I became interested in family therapy, it started to become clear that with the sorts of problems children were facing we needed to look towards the broader systems as well. Early on in my career I became involved with children who had experienced abuse and also with those who were understood to be delinquent. Just working with families in these circumstances was never enough. We needed to be working with schools, with the police, with magistrates, with after school care and so on. I was drawn to the idea that we had to engage with these systems, that we had to work systemically.

The work of the Milan team was a significant influence at this time. I loved the way this team was so neutral and in many ways so creative about what was happening for families. Their approach tended to offer people a lot of dignity and that attracted me to this form of family therapy. It showed to me that there were different ways of approaching people and validating their experience. We did not need to tell them that what they were doing was wrong. We didn't need to instruct them or give them advice but could, through questioning, explore their ways of living, their solutions and their ideas about ways of moving forward.

These were the early influences on my work. Subsequently I got very involved with Kensington Consultation Centre, and Peter Lang in particular, and together we have been very interested in social constructionist ideas, stimulated by contact with Vernon Cronen and Barnett Pearce. These ideas invite considerations about our responsibility as therapists in how we contribute to the construction of reality in our conversations. In a different way, the changes to the health service in Britain meant that we had to develop ways of working with families that would bring quick results. This was a far cry from the idea of psychoanalytic long-term engagements.

A further key thought involved our concern that if we took children out of school, out of their normal environment, that it is possible this can create more problems for them. We began to look for moral and ethical ways of acting to create a speed of change – both for economic reasons, but more importantly for the sake of the children and the families.

Did this contribute to your interest in appreciative inquiry?

Yes, although there were a number of strands that all converged at the same time. We soon realised that the children we were seeing in therapy had generally come to regard themselves as 'bad', 'naughty', and that they were seeing us because they had 'misbehaved' in some way. It seemed obvious to us that we all really grow from positivity, from being affirmed, from being understood and from having our abilities seen, heard and appreciated. We were searching for ways to bring forth people's, as yet, unseen strengths and abilities. We wanted to find ways of working in therapy that would enable people to see that they already have the skills and competence to go on and to address the difficulties in their lives. Bringing out the values evident within a family gives them dignity and an energy to go on. Another strand at the time involved my love of sport. I play a lot of sport and have always had an interest in how sports people are trained. All the learning in sport comes from being shown what you do right, not being shown what you do wrong. So we learn from what we are already doing well or right and need encouragement to do more of it. Thirdly and importantly, at about this time we met David Cooperrider and Diane Whitney and began to learn about their ideas of appreciative enquiry as applied to communities and organisational development. That took us to a different focus and stimulated us to work with the schools and children within a community. Through a process of questioning, abilities, skills, resources and values of the members of that community are brought forth and then, fired with a sense of their own competence, everyone begins to dream or imagine how their community could be.

How did your focus come to be so strongly on people's futures rather than their pasts?

In working with children what seemed clear to us was that they are desperately excited about and driven by their futures. We began to explore how ideas about the future powerfully create the present and certainly present action. Of course the past is important, but we have begun to focus on working with the future. We see every problem as a frustrated dream; a hope that something could be different, so we work with the difference or the dream not the problem. We've loved to work within the metaphor of dreams. Wittgenstein's ideas about language games have been important to us. We believe that speaking within the realm of dreams takes people into a certain sort of language game – one that brings energy, creativity, play, hope and excitement. Dreams are also fragmentary. You can work on different parts of the dream in each conversation. Dreams can also change and it doesn't matter if they don't come true, because dreams often don't. One can at least get part of the way towards the fulfilment of the dream and this can be significant.

Our focus on dream talk has been informed by appreciative inquiry work, and also by Boscolo's work in relation to talking about the future, and Peggy Penn's future questioning. We now focus much more on the future and future dreaming very early on in our conversations with people. We ask people what they are good at, proud of, enjoy, and as they talk we name their abilities and values, as these will generate the energy for fulfilling their dreams. As John Dewey describes, future hopes create our actions in the present.

Could you talk about how these ideas have translated into your conversations with people? Could you give an example perhaps?

Perhaps I can offer the example of a young girl whom I was working with who had experienced abuse. She walked into my office as a very large girl with shaved hair, tattoos on her head, and I don't think she had showered for a week. I had been asked to see her because she was so angry. She clearly didn't want to come and see an expletive expletive expletive shrink. She was very angry at being there. I just said to her, 'You've talked to everybody about your past. Let's talk about your dreams for the future.' And her whole face just lit up as she said her dream was to become a princess. In my mind I could not think of two more opposite visions – but I took her very seriously. I asked her what the concept of princess meant for her. Wittgenstein's ideas about language games and the meaning of a word being created in how it is used, have been very important to us, as it has helped us join the other person's grammar. This means we really try to understand what they are saying and what the words they are using mean to them. We have created the idea of 'linguagrams' (like a mind map) where we jointly explore in detail the meanings, actions, emotions, moral orders and intentionality of significant words. In this case it was the word 'princess'.

She started talking about being a people's princess who would do things for other people, who would be caring and generous, and a beautiful ambassador. She described a princess who was slender and well dressed. Over the next few months we started talking about what this princess would be doing. I discovered that, while this girl was fourteen years old and hadn't been attending school for a long time, the princess was a social worker. We ventured into the realm of the future in our conversations. I said, 'Okay it is now ten years' time and you have trained as a social worker. What university did you go to?' She mentioned one in the north of England. I asked, 'What did you read there?' She said 'I don't know, psychology and sociology and a few other things like that.' Then I said, 'Do you remember when you were 14? You'd been out of school for two or three years. Do you remember how you got back in to school?' She said, 'I had this very nice psychiatrist who helped me'. I said, 'How did she help you?' And she started talking about how we had made a phone call to the school. I said, 'Who spoke? Did you or her?' She replied, 'The psychiatrist spoke but she arranged a meeting for us to go to the school'. I said, 'Do you remember how you shook hands with the head teacher when you went in? And how you looked and gave her fantastic eye contact? Do you remember what you wore?' We went into these minute details about what that particular meeting was like – looking from the future back. And she was able to describe the conversations that we had had, how confident she had been, how well she had spoken, and the subjects she had talked about. I didn't say anymore about it.

About a month after this conversation she said to me, 'I think it's about time we went to the school don't you. Can you ring and make an appointment?' I asked if she needed to talk about it anymore and she said no, that she knew how to behave.

When we went into the school she was just brilliant. I first met that girl roughly ten years ago. Now she is a qualified social worker. She fulfilled her dream – although she didn't go to the university she mentioned.

We didn't talk about her past at all, until one day she rang me up and cancelled her appointment and said she'd like to meet me in town. She said that she was no longer a patient but she wanted me to help her choose some clothes. Her mother suffered from schizophrenia and her father had abused her and was in prison, so I guess I had become a bit of a substitute mum. We went around to the various shops and while we were doing this I said, 'It has always interested me, why do you want to be a princess?' I had some idea why this might be the case and I thought it might be good to have a conversation about it. She said, 'because that's what my dad always called me'. We then had a conversations about whether she was going to be her dad's princess or her own princess. We spoke about what her own princess was going to be and how this was different from her dad's princess. But that was the only talk that we had about the abusive relationship. She taught me a huge amount about the power of future talk. We still meet up at times and she offers me advice about my work with other children who have experienced abuse. It is just lovely.

Talking about the future in these ways gives hope and a sense that there is a future for these young people. It also offers ways for them to act in the present. It avoids offering prescriptions about what they are going to do and how they ought to do it. There was certainly not much point me encouraging this young woman to go to school. Everyone she knew had been trying to do so with no results. But looking at her future dreams, hopes and values and working backwards opened different possibilities. It was also playful and fanciful and if it hadn't happened it would not have been seen as failing as it was only a dream.

I know that you have also been doing preventive work in schools, can you speak a little bit about this?

We have become very interested in how we can contribute to creating futures for young people, particularly those young people who are in families who find it difficult to come to what are basically middle-class facilities and therapists. I am passionate about appreciative inquiry work with school children and their communities. This work involves training children to interview each other about things they are really excited about, things they are proud of, things that give them joy and hope, and their dreams about the future. We train children to ask in detail about these high points and from these stories they pick out the other children's abilities, skills, values and hopes. Sometimes we write each of these abilities on little 'post-its' or stickers that the children wear for the day, giving them new identities to be proud of: 'creative, helpful, imaginative, competent, courageous'. Ricoeur talks about our identities being created through the stories others tell of us. This has, therefore, become a very active way of getting positive stories told of people (raising self esteem). This is important both for the person and those they relate to, as there are now witnesses to these stories. There is both a desire and an expectation to fulfil the new identities and allow the abilities to grow. These stories come from the detailed description of already lived episodes, so there is a validity to them, it isn't just flattery.

All their abilities and skills can be written down and taken home to be placed on the fridge. Every time they fulfil one of their abilities they mark it up and watch their abilities grow! We have found that these little children just love this process. It has also been a way of linking with families and schools in deprived areas. Sometimes in these communities we have asked the children to interview their parents. Not only does this improve the dialogue and relationships within the family, but it also engenders a greater sense of belonging and pride while collecting and telling the class about the many resources present in their family. In situations where there have been problems between young people and the elderly, the young people have gone out to interview the elders, to gather stories of the elders' achievements or pride and then retell these stories in the schools. These actions have generated a lot more community spirit. A 'borrow a grand-parent scheme' arose from such interviews, giving lonely single parents an opportunity to both belong but also to go out. Much of this work in schools has been inspired by the work of David Cooperrider and Bliss Browne in their appreciative inquiry projects in Chicago.

If you were to do a quick appreciative inquiry of the family therapy field at this point in time what would you see? What futures of the field do you feel most hopeful about?

I think one of things that has struck me at this conference that has been really exciting and impressive is that people are really not just working with families. The Just Therapy Group from Lower Hutt, New Zealand, for example are demonstrating the importance of working with policy and research. I think this is part of a broader realisation that we as family therapists are a part of the community and that we have a responsibility to play our part in changing the structures and discourses around us. A lot of the workshops I have been to over the last few days have been very much looking at how we as therapists can have an effect on the wider systems that influence families, and how we can create space for voices, that have for so long been silenced, to be heard. I think these are some of the current considerations for the field and I believe this is really exciting. We have moved a long way from seeing individuals as pathological. Now we are not only looking at the relationships between those individuals and their families, but also at the society at large and I think that is really hopeful.

13

Family stories

an interview with

John Byng-Hall

As a past Chair of the Institute of Family Therapy, and as the author of a wide range of articles and books including 'Rewriting Family Scripts', John Byng-Hall has for many years been an influential figure in family therapy. This interview took place at John's home in London. Cheryl White and David Denborough were present. David was the interviewer.

To begin these interviews, I've often asked people how they first came to be engaged with family therapy, and we've traced some of the diverse histories that brought people into this field. Would this be a good place to start?

Yes, I think so. I'm semi-retired now and I'm just in the process of writing my life story in one continuous flow. It's like telling a story to myself and I'm finding it fascinating, disturbing, and quite painful all at the same time. At this stage I have just written about my earlier years which took place in Kenya, Africa. I was born there and lived on a farm in the Rift Valley.

I've heard that is just a beautiful part of the world ...

Oh yes. The house we were brought up in was called Flamingo House which was located between two lakes. We were at the highest point between the two lakes and every evening when the flamingos were there they would fly over our house. Tens of thousands of them in V formation. I don't know if you are aware, but the underside of a flamingo's wings are a deep brilliant scarlet colour, and they make an extraordinary noise when they fly together. They have these long slender necks and every evening at sunset we would see these birds flying about twenty feet above us. That was an everyday part of my childhood. I thought that was what happened everywhere. The Rift Valley was about forty miles across, there were volcanoes on the bottom, including the second biggest volcano in the world. And the sides of the valley went up dramatically to the highlands of Kenya, up to 10,000 feet in some places. It was a quite amazing place to live.

I grew up hearing stories from my father, who was born in Zimbabwe, of similar beauty, but also of the complexities of living as a white person in southern Africa. You mentioned that in your writings some of the stories are disturbing and painful. Do these relate to these complexities?

Some of the stories that I have found painful to write have concerned a friendship with an African of my age. There were a number of poignant moments that took place as the Mau Mau were beginning their rebellion against colonisation. As the rebellion began, my African friend, with whom I used to go hunting, took me to a clearing in the forest where there was a dog hanging in the middle of the clearing. This was the signature of the Mau Mau. I could hear sounds in the forest. It was my friend's way of warning me that troubles were ahead. We were thirteen at the time.

As teenagers we had many shared ideals and common heroes. One of these was a white 25 year old son of the next door neighbour. We would talk in admiration about him. Then one day, not long after my friend's warning, the news came that this next door neighbour had been killed by the Mau Mau. Shortly afterwards, we were in the stables and caught each other's eye over the back of a horse. At that moment we suddenly knew that we were on opposite sides. It was a moment I have never forgotten. I still see the picture in my mind. It was terribly upsetting.

It wasn't until later that I discovered that my friend had then gone off to join the Mau Mau and I know this was the right thing for him to do. I don't know what came of him. He had a very common name and it was very hard to trace. But also, there was then a terrific gulf between people like me and people like him. I have never forgotten him though, nor that moment between us.

There must, I imagine, be so many stories in the world like that one of yours and your friend. And I imagine those events were influential in shaping some aspects of your life. Did they in some way contribute to you working in the areas that you have?

Growing up in Africa, my family was often thrown together with survival as an issue, and so family life was highly significant to me. As a white family, we were very isolated which made me long for connections with those around me. The friendship I just spoke about was an example of how one can cross the boundaries but how difficult that can also be. This is a theme which has constantly been present in my work as a family therapist. But there was another event that led me eventually to family therapy.

In 1956 I was leaving Kenya to travel by boat to Cambridge University where I was going to study agricultural science, to become a farmer. But when the boat was passing through the Suez Canal I became sick. It wasn't until the ship was in the Mediterranean that polio was diagnosed and I had to be taken off the ship in southern Italy. I was paralysed from the waist down.

Living with the effects of polio made the idea of becoming a farmer impossible. Luckily though, the pre-requisites to get into agriculture, which I had fulfilled, were the same as were needed for medicine. I was allowed to come to Cambridge and study medicine.

I actually started thinking about working with families when I was a medical student, in 1961, reading the work of Bowlby. This was where the seeds for my future were sown as I found his writings about attachment very enlightening and this made me want to work with him eventually. In some ways it could be said that Bowlby did the first family therapy work in the late 1940s when he would consult with families in situations in which workers had become stuck with an individual. Bowlby has been the greatest single influence on my work. I came to know him very well in his retirement and I really admire him.

But there were many influences here in the UK in relation to the development of family therapy. Here there was an atmosphere of engaging with many different ideas rather than a development of separate schools of family therapy. One of the most important innovations of the time was that you could actually watch people working with families. People would show their videotapes and also their live interviews. Prior to this, people would only tell stories of their work. It was very exciting watching each other work and we went through enthusiasms in watching Sal Minuchin, the Milan team, Olga Silverstein, Peggy Papp, Don Bloch and many others. All of these family therapists would be invited to the UK and we would organise conferences and workshops with them. The ideas were stunning, and there was a whole atmosphere of exploration and discovery. Looking back, it was an enlivening and enriching time.

Could you say a little bit about your work during these early years of family therapy?

During these times I was working as a consultant with the Tavistock Clinic here in London seeing families, teaching and supervising and setting up the Family Therapy Program. The Family Therapy Program at the Tavistock, and the Family Institute in Cardiff, were the first places to set up family therapy training programs in the UK. But I was also working for Camden Social Services in an assessment unit for children who had received court orders to place them in the care of local authority. My job would involve meeting with these children and their parents and siblings in the family homes. I used to go in to these homes and our meetings would unfold at the pace the families could manage. I'd try to persuade the parents to turn the television off and ask to see the family photographs. I'd try to build a meaningful relationship with the parents who were usually angry that the courts had taken their children away. The children would accompany us for these meetings, as would the social workers who were working with the children. The parents were usually furious at first and this was understandable. But on the second visit I would often say: 'Well look, you know, I'm going to have to write this report, what do you suggest we do?' We would eventually begin to work out some forms of collaboration and some plans of action. These two half-day home visits were incredibly moving and often we got very engaged with the families. The interesting thing was that the number of children's homes went from thirty-four when I started down to two. In other words, once we had developed these ways of working with families we were usually able to avoid the children going into care. Of course this was the time when there was a switch from residential to foster care, so this was also a major factor in why the children's homes were being closed down. Nonetheless, I believe that developing ways of working with families at these moments of crisis, when courts had become involved in relation to the care of children, did make a significant difference.

I know that you have always been interested in family stories. Can you say a little about your interest in this area?

Yes, the first paper that I wrote about family stories was in 1979. I've always been interested in how family stories are told, how they're listened to, and who tells them. I've also been interested in how family legends about the past can encode rules about how family members should be behaving now. These rules are conveyed in the attitudes about what has happened in the past. In working with families I ask quite a bit about what happens between sessions, and when the family members tell me their stories about this, I then work with these. The idea is to eventually enable the family members to become more aware of the implications of their family stories. My interest in Bowlby's theories of attachment plays a large part in how I understand the stories that people are telling.

It's probably important to note that despite my interest in stories and family narratives, I do not see myself as someone who utilises a 'narrative approach' to therapy, nor do I consider myself a 'narrative therapist' as the term is currently used in the field. Rather, I believe that all therapy consists of narrative, as therapists and families talk to each other, and all therapists may benefit from appreciating the function of narrative elements in their work. With Renos Papadopoulos, I have recently edited a book entitled 'Multiple Voices: Narrative in systemic family psychotherapy' in which the staff members of the Family Therapy Group at the Tavistock explore how understandings of narrative and story can enhance the work and practice of family therapy. The way a family story is heard and responded to moulds the story itself. A family discussion provides a context in which everyone is both narrator and listener, and as family therapists we join this process. By listening for what can be linked together, we as therapists can play a part in eliciting a more coherent story about the family's predicaments. To do this, however, I believe the therapist needs ideas about what constitutes coherent and incoherent narrative. As I've already mentioned, I find attachment research very helpful in this regard. Mary Main researched what makes a coherent narrative by studying the stories told by individuals about their past childhood. She and her colleagues found that if they told a coherent story about their past attachments they were more likely to have secure attachments with their children.

The stories you told earlier of your childhood friendships in Kenya have reminded me of how I would like to have more conversations with my father about his experiences of growing up in Africa. The stories you told were powerful to me. Are these the sorts of family stories that you would consider may become family legends?

Well, come to think of it, yes! The stories that I have been telling you today have been part of the stories I have told my family over a long period. The ways I have been telling them to you will add a further step in the re-editing of these stories in what is a long and interesting process.

Thanks John. It's been great to speak with you.

14

The Public Conversations Project

an interview with

Sallyann Roth

Sallyann Roth is one of the principal facilitators and trainers of the Public Conversations Project – a project that is exploring the use of family therapy skills and techniques to foster dialogue as an alternative to debate on divisive public issues. Other principal facilitators and trainers of the project currently include: Corky Becker, Laura Chasin, Richard Chasin, Bill Madsen and Bob Stains. The Project's website is www.publicconversations.org

The following interview took place at the Family Therapy World Congress in Oslo where Sallyann was presenting on the topic 'Preparing to meet the other: A step toward reconciliation'.

Sallyann, I was wondering whether you could speak a little about the origins of The Public Conversations Project.

In 1989 Laura Chasin was disturbed by televised 'debates' – exchanges in which people were verbally violent, yelled, talked over each other, made personal attacks, and did not listen to, or even seem especially interested in, each other. She noticed that this kind of exchange – lots of heat and little light – was the kind that people in conflict regularly bring to our therapy offices. Would it be possible, she wondered, to transfer the skills we use in private, clinical conversations to conflicts that take place in the public arena? A group of us began meeting at lunch to turn over ideas about this. After some great discussions we decided we could answer this question only by moving into action.

We decided that we would focus on people who were in conflict in an area that had political or social significance; we were committed to exploring ways to facilitate good, contactful conversations among people experiencing such conflict. We became an action-research project.

The first people we met with were pro-life and pro-choice activists who were divided over the issue of abortion. This topic involved value and worldview differences, it was a bona fide chronic and stuck conflict, and we had ready access to deeply committed people on both 'sides'. At any rate, because of our anxieties about what it would be like to bring these people together, or perhaps simply because of our inexperience, we first met with these groups of people separately. Both groups told us that they really wanted to talk with people on the other side. We asked the people in each initial group to give us advice about what would make a different, a better, kind of conversation possible, and when we got to bringing the 'opponents' together, we took their advice. One person said, 'Don't sit us on opposite sides from our opponents; let us sit next to each other – within touching distance'. Another said, 'Don't let them call us names we would not call ourselves'. They got us started thinking about arrangements for the seating, and the elaboration of agreements or ground rules for the meeting. This was the beginning of our idea that we were partnered with participants in the conversation to see what all of us could do to make a different kind of conversation possible.

In our current work, we have an individual pre-meeting contact with all participants to establish and develop their intentions for themselves in the meeting, and to learn about what conditions we (and they) can create to make achieving their own intentions more, rather than less, likely. These pre-meeting conversations aren't one-way conversations in which we are told about peoples' wishes and needs for the forthcoming conversation. They are collaborative, two-way conversations in which peoples' intentions become elaborated and developed through inquiry and listening, as do their commitments to those intentions. As we talk with potential participants about why they want to converse with people they experience as disturbingly different, their intentions, whatever they may have been, always evolve beyond win/lose paradigms toward ideas about why they might want to listen to what those 'others' have to say.

We take what we have learned from the potential participants into account in designing and facilitating the meeting that follows. We always structure meetings to encourage reflection, personal speaking, and inquiry, and to discourage automatic reactivity around the issue at hand. Meetings are highly structured in the beginning. We want people to have an unusual, personal, connecting, and reflective experience of themselves and each other before they move to more free-form conversation.

Practical details about the kinds of structures we develop are specific to each group we meet with, although the principles that guide us in developing a meeting design are reliably the same. These are described on our website (www.publicconversations. org).

Toward the end of each meeting, we ask people to comment on how they experienced the meeting and their participation in it. Later, we also call everyone up for even more feedback. From participants' reflections we hear what has worked well for them, what hasn't, and their suggestions for future meetings. We also hear about other reflections they have from a more distant perspective. We take what they tell us, along with our own observations and reflections, into the design of our next dialogue.

Can you say a little about the types of different public conflicts you have worked with?

Well, as I said, we have facilitated many conversations with pro-choice and pro-life activists on the issue of abortion. And also with:

- Leaders of organisations involved in population and in women's health who were struggling over their disparate goals for the 1994 United Nations Conference on Population and Development.

- Private land owners, ecologists, private citizens, and lumber company representatives in conflicts about the Northern New England Forest.

- Members of a small city government on developing a more appreciative climate around issues of race and class.

- Students at one school and parents, staff, and teachers at another, around economic difference or class difference, however they defined it.

- Members of the US Congress in a bi-partisan retreat.

- People divided over issues about prison labour.

- Leaders of a major Protestant denomination around issues of sexuality and homosexuality within the church.

Although we hope that these conversations about public issues will eventually affect the ways the conflicts are being handled in the public arena, most of our conversations have started out in private.

This is not a complete list, but I am sure it gives you an idea of the scope of issues we've worked with. We are sometimes seen as the people who hold abortion dialogues. We prefer to be seen as the people who work with people in conflicts that have a high social cost, are longstanding, and seemingly unmoveable, that tear our communities apart.

We never expect people to change their views in these conversations; people come because they know we are not asking them to change their minds or positions. They come to hear and to be heard, to learn and to connect. We hope the meetings provide a structure that encourages the kind of contact that increases people's sense of community and common humanity, and that reduces stereotyping and dehumanisation of the 'other'.

From all these attempts to create the context for useful conversations between people who are in public disagreement, what have been some of the key learnings?

One key learning is that in order for these conversations to be effective, most of the work has to be done prior to the meeting. We have recently been developing ways to circulate certain pre-meeting information among the group of participants so that they are working as a group as well as individuals before they get to the actual meeting. Another key learning is to value and respect how much time it takes to be truly collaborative in the design of each meeting so that all of us feel like we own the process and have a big investment in how it comes out. I have become passionate (as have we all) about developing even more ways for people to experience – and get curious about and interested in – what they don't know about others that they felt they knew, or might have been afraid to know.

In terms of that initial aim of family therapists using their skills in the public arena, how has that interchange happened – not only in terms of family therapy skills being used to address issues in the public arena, but also how this process has influenced your family therapy practices?

At first we had the idea that leaders of opposing groups could not shift the ways they talked with each other (even in a private context) without feeling they were risking their positions in their organisations, or in the public eye. So early on, we avoided working with leaders. We have changed our views on that. We learned that leaders in totally private contexts could make shifts – not in their position on the issue, whatever it might be, but in their relationships to each other. We really listen to the people in a group or organisation who are connected around the issues, to sort out what the most accessible and effective point of leverage might be – leaders, community members, or some other group altogether. In the beginning, the first question is, 'Should there be a conversation?' and the next is, 'Who should come?' We have seen remarkable outcomes from some of these conversations.

What has all this meant for our therapy practices? Well, some of us have stopped doing therapy altogether to participate in the project full time. Those of us who still do therapy have changed our practices a lot. I now do much more collaborative work up front with families before we meet about what might ensure a successful therapy process and whether it makes sense to go ahead with meeting. If we can't come up with some shared, over-arching intention for the meeting, or if everyone can't sign on to why it is worth really listening to everybody else, then I don't go ahead. We have put a lot of thought into how to invite people to be their 'best listeners' as well as their 'best speakers' in the PCP meetings, and we have set up very clear specifications about speaking and listening turns. I have transferred these ideas into my clinical practice. I know that my colleagues in the project have more and different things to say, as well.

What were some of the things about being family therapists that would have particularly contributed to going in this direction? And what family therapy skills have influenced the Public Conversations Project?

In the field of people who work with conflict, for years people talked about conflict 'resolution'. But this description didn't hold up because the kind of conflict we are talking about involves people's identities, values, and worldviews, and these are never 'resolved'. They are constantly changing. Then the field started to change and people began to talk about conflict 'management' as if we as professionals could do something to manage the conflict. This also seems rather unrealistic! In the last three or four years the idea of conflict 'transformation' has become more popular. This description acknowledges that a conflict may continue, but how people deal with it and what meanings are attributed to it, can shift. It fits with the idea that explicating different meanings people have about their lives and working with people's separate life stories can enable transformations. As family therapists, we were used to attending to different people's stories and their meanings. We were also used to not moving to a single view, but instead creating room for people to live in good connection to each other, with their differences. And we never expected that differences would be 'resolved' or that it was our job to 'manage' them. As therapists, and as facilitators, we don't expect that the work we do will transform either the people or the problem. We believe that the most successful conversations transform the family members' or participants' relationships to the differences between them, transform their relationships to how that difference has been played out, transform their relationships to each other, and most important, I think, transform what care, love, and connection they experience as possible in a world filled with difference.

Sitting as we are in the plenary hall of this Family Therapy World Congress, what would you see as some of the issues that the field of family therapy is grappling with? What are you most excited by?

While I have been here, I have really enjoyed hearing Elspeth McAdam and Peter Lang, whose work with dreaming into the future and with language continues to be catalytic for me. I am most excited by those therapies that focus on people's preferences and their dreams. Ongoing developments in narrative therapy also continue to offer new challenges. I have been inspired by the work of Arild Aambo and Tahira Iqbal, along with their colleagues. They are changing the shape of 'professionalism' through their creative reliance on natural helpers in service delivery to (and capacity building within) the Somali and Pakistani immigrant communities in Norway. Nora Sveaass (of Norway) presented work she did with Marcia Castillo (of Nicaragua) showing the value of – no, the necessity for – a socio-political frame for therapeutic understanding and action in a post-war, social reconstruction situation. I will be thinking about the implications of their work for a good long time.

There is also some exciting work happening in relation to redefining family. I am struggling to find language that describes what we are doing in much broader ways. Perhaps one day we will not even use the word 'family' because that word itself is very constricting. We are working with significant groups of people who are connected to each other – but that is not exactly catchy language! In all of my work I don't think of the word 'family' – I don't think narrowly in terms of family. I think more the way that Harlene Anderson and Harry Goolishian were thinking years ago: Who are the people involved around this issue?

To my mind, the most creative work is being done by those who cross fields. There is wonderful work from philosophers, linguists, cultural critics, and anthropologists that has an enormous amount to offer family therapy. Without these fresh influences we run the risk of simply repeating what has gone before.

15

Addressing our own practices of power

an interview with

Karl Tomm

Karl Tomm is a Professor of Psychiatry at Calgary University, Canada. Karl teaches internationally and is widely respected. His writings and teachings have contributed richly to the field of family therapy. The following interview took place at the Family Therapy World Congress in Oslo where Karl was giving a keynote presentation on the topic: 'Reconciliation in clinical work'.

Could we begin with what you see as some of the broad themes that make up family therapy? I'm interested in why you believe people are gathering at a conference like this around the emblem of family therapy ...

Family relationships are probably the most complex and intense relationships that people have in their lifetime, and the field of family therapy reflects the significance of these relationships. The focus that family therapy has placed on patterns of interaction in relationship has been extremely valuable. It has validated the importance of the human experience of relatedness and connectedness. I think these themes make up one core of family therapy.

Some of the more recent developments in the field that focus on language and meaning have also been important. Language is first learnt in family interaction and it is through language that people give meaning to their life experiences. What we aim to do as family therapists is to facilitate preferred directions of interaction and preferred meanings in relationships.

What have been some of the historical steps that have led to this emphasis on relationship?

It was a realisation about the importance of the relationship context of people's lives that began the family therapy initiative in the 1940s and 1950s. As people began to look at the context of people's lives they began to think of families in terms of systems which have certain boundaries and coherence within those boundaries.

One of the big changes in the field occurred towards the late 1970s and early 1980s when there was a shift from what I would describe as a first order perspective, to a second order perspective. The first order perspective entailed attempts to understand the family system as separate from the therapist, so that we could objectively operate upon it to try to facilitate behavioural change, whereas the second order perspective includes the therapist as a participant in the meaning making process, co-constructing ideas, beliefs and realities. The second order perspective regards behavioural change as secondary to changes in understanding. There were various other changes in focus as well but these were some of the most significant.

The early 1980s became a watershed period as a lot of people began immersing themselves in a second order perspective. To me, the recent approaches to family therapy that have become popular are all second order approaches. The Milan systemic approach (of Boscolo and Cecchin), the collaborative language systems approach (of Goolishian and Anderson), the solution focused approach (of de Shazer and Berg), and the narrative approach (of White and Epston), in my view are all second order approaches. These stand in contrast to some of the more traditional models like strategic therapy and structural family therapy which represent first order approaches. These are generalisations but I think they reflect relevant distinctions.

I would say that one of the big challenges facing the field now is how to address larger social issues of unequal power and social injustice, and how the language, meanings and practices used by families themselves are informed by cultural processes and beliefs. As part of this cultural process we are now seeing ourselves as professionals as vulnerable to getting caught in power dynamics that are pathologising, or alternatively responding to these relations of power in ways that enable constructive change. Working through some of these issues is where I see the field right now.

Would you be interested in talking a little bit about where you were in relation to your own work when the thinking was moving between first order and second order perspectives? What sorts of issues were you working on at the time? And what sort of differences did the changes in the broader field make to your thinking and work?

My initial orientation to therapy developed from working within the McMaster problem-solving approach. I was also influenced by the work of Salvador Minuchin and Jay Haley. I tried to integrate their ideas with cybernetic concepts from Gregory Bateson and the MRI, and eventually developed my own version of a first order approach which I called 'circular pattern diagramming'. It was actually a significant failure experience that I had with a family I was working with, which opened space for me to reflect critically upon my work and to think more broadly. I had used all of the ideas and methods from the models I just described with this particular family. Despite my best efforts, the father committed suicide. I sought out new ideas after this experience and what I came across at that time was the work of the Milan team and their book 'Paradox and Counter Paradox'. It was the hunger to learn from my mistakes and the process of vigorously exploring their work that made it possible for me to make a shift from a first order to a second order perspective.

Being trained as a physician, I was more heavily invested in empirical ways of viewing things than some, but when I made the shift to a second order perspective I had to abandon this. Letting go of assumptions about objectivity was extremely difficult but important for me. From there, it has been a very exciting process that has led in all sorts of directions. Some of the explorations in my recent clinical work have included developing what I refer to as 'internalised-other interviewing', while much of my current personal attention is focused on how to become aware of my own patterns of perpetrating social injustice and trying to address these as best I can.

Can you say a little bit more about this in the context of how you see the field trying to grapple with these sorts of issues?

If we take seriously the idea that many of the mental difficulties that persons in families experience arise to a certain extent, or even to a major extent, through social processes of unfairness and injustice, then we need to pay attention to those larger social processes and not only work with individual families. One analogy I like to use is the epidemiological approach of community medicine. If you are dealing with an epidemic of say diarrhoea, it is important to treat individual cases, to treat actual patients, but it is also important to do something about the source of the infection in the community. If the water supply is known to be contaminated with toxic bacteria, then to deal only with individual cases of illness could involve questionable ethics. We would be profiting from the illness that is being generated in the wider community. If we assume that social injustices are a major source of family and individual turmoil, then we also have to pay attention to these social issues and not just work with individual cases because we profit from that. My view is that we have an ethical imperative to devote at least a portion of our time to addressing these social issues. And one of the main ways I do this is through teaching – to try to invite people to think about these ideas, to pay attention to them. There are of course many other ways to be involved in these issues, for instance through direct social action.

One of the things you were teaching about yesterday was about broadening out the ideas of perpetrator-hood. Can you speak a little about this?

I think it is very hard for us to recognise our own patterns of collusion. So that, while it is quite common to deconstruct victim-hood and look at primary, secondary and tertiary victims of situations, we rarely do so in relation to perpetrator-ship. I have tried to look at deconstructing perpetrator-ship at three levels: primary perpetrators are those who themselves commit a particular injustice; secondary perpetrators are those who are complicit in some direct or indirect way; and tertiary perpetrators are those who collude with the values and ways of thinking in a community that make the unfair actions possible. Examples of tertiary perpetrator-ship include collusion with sexist, racist or homophobic beliefs and practices.

Through these reflections I have come to realise how limited my personal development has been in addressing my own participation in social injustices and living coherently within a position of, for example, anti-sexism. I have been struggling with the issue of unfair gender relations for many years and coming to greater and greater awareness about the issues and practices involved, but still on many occasions examples of my ongoing sexism are drawn to my attention by various women and men. Rather than turning away from these examples of my tertiary perpetratorship, I believe they, and my feelings of regret about them, can be a generative source of change and restorative action.

Let me take for example my German ethnic heritage and the Holocaust. I was talking to a Jewish friend last week about this, and although I don't feel it is coherent for me to apologise for the Holocaust, as I was not directly involved, I do feel it is important to think through how I am connected to those events. Through my German background, the values of anti-Semitism were part of the community in which I was raised. Insofar as I, in any way, consciously or unconsciously, contribute to supporting anti-Semitism I collude in the practices that made the Holocaust possible. For this I can apologise. By acknowledging the profound injustices that occurred, and expressing deep regret and remorse for what my people have done, it makes it easier for me to make a stronger stand against anti-Semitism in my everyday life. For me to work with, rather than deny, my guilt feelings, I can find ways of using these feelings in ways that I think are constructive. I am involved in exploring the nuances of perpetratorship like this and being able to do something about my participation in these processes.

What would your hope be about these explorations? What might they make possible both in your work personally and also in the field of family therapy?

My hope would be to move in the direction of less violence and more respect and to contribute to patterns of interaction that promote healing and wellness. There is so much continuing violence in the world that human respect is something that needs to be continually regenerated and revitalised.

There are many dilemmas in promoting this however. In my presentation yesterday, I spoke about traditions of forgiveness and how I view these as desirable in comparison to those of revenge. But the notion of forgiveness is emphasised in the Christian tradition, more so than in other religions. My worry is that by speaking about forgiveness in the ways that I did that it could be a way of me exercising 'Christian privilege'. This could be problematic if I am implicitly propagating Christian values and imposing them on people who have other religious beliefs. In my work with families I would own a preference for forgiveness rather than philosophies of retribution such as 'an eye for an eye and a tooth for a tooth'. I think it was Gandhi who said that if we all lived by such a philosophy the world would be blind and toothless!! But there are legitimate criticisms about the ways in which forgiveness is sometimes evoked. It is sometimes spoken about in ways that ignore complexities. For instance, to push someone who is not ready to forgive is to perpetuate a further violation These are issues that I believe the field of family therapy needs to grapple with.

Issues of forgiveness and perpetrator-ship certainly infuse many conversations within therapy rooms. Are there other issues that you feel the field of family therapy needs to address?

Somehow as a field I believe we are going to have to grapple with the current thrust towards medicalising the entire mental health field. Some of the ideas that are emerging in relation to this trend are very disturbing. There is a belief emerging amongst some psychiatrists that people with schizophrenia need to be treated with medication early on in life as a way to prevent a subtle deterioration process in the brain. The related medical practice, encouraged by drug companies, is to identify such people early, put them on medication and keep them on medication for their entire life. I do not yet know the literature in this area in depth but I find the line of reasoning quite frightening.

I am also concerned about the degree to which we as professionals are vulnerable to being caught up in the power of medicine, psychiatry and professionalism. In Canada, the discipline of psychiatry is the most dominant in decision-making about mental health services in the community. Currently, psychiatric residents don't get a lot of training in working with people psychologically or socially. I think this is really sad. It means they become primarily interested in medical approaches and psychopharmacology. While I see this as a very troubling development, I remain hopeful because I believe that family therapy has significant potential to offer alternative ways of working.

There are also some developments within our own field that are cause for concern. One of the dangers in how the family therapy field has developed and embraced systems theory is that the tendency to label – which the DSM does for individuals – has been transferred to families. Terms such as dysfunctional families, or psychosomatic families, or disengaged families, are labels that stigmatise and demean. Other diagnostic terms have been developed out of some of the more recent complex instruments for assessing families. This to me is seriously problematic. We need to find other ways of thinking about social processes and dynamics that avoid the negative effects of labelling. There is a lot more work that needs to be done in this regard so that we don't inadvertently perpetrate subtle patterns of social injustice in our relations with the individuals and families who seek our help.

16

Talking about complexities

an interview with

Marcia Sheinberg

Marcia Sheinberg is the Director of Training and Clinical Services at the Ackerman Institute for the Family. She is also an advisory editor for the influential journal Family Process. This interview took place at the Ackerman Institute. Cheryl White and David Denborough were present. David was the interviewer.

The field has just welcomed the release of your book (written with Peter Fraenkel), 'The Relational Trauma of Incest: A family-based approach to treatment'. I look forward to talking with you about this aspect of your work, but first, I'd like to ask you about how you came to be working as a therapist. When you were young, was this an area that you would have imagined working in?

That's a question I can only really answer by speaking a little about my family background. My father emigrated from Russia when he was seventeen, and my mother left Transylvania when she was nine and they were certainly very interesting parents. I grew up in an experimental community based on socialist principles which was founded during the depression of the 1930s as a haven for the garment workers of New York City. There were 200 families and we all had the same type of cinder-block house with a flat-roof. We each had a half-acre of land to grow vegetables and between these plots was common land. All houses faced land rather than other houses. This was supposed to enable us to commune with nature. In the beginning the people were supposed to farm together and share money, but this concept of a socialist community did not last for very long. However, the community began to attract artists until it became a gathering place for factory workers, writers and artists.

My parents joined this community after the socialist idea had failed, but they were attracted to its ideals and its history. The people were working-class and very progressive for the most part, although later there was a terrible divide in the community during the Macarthy era when people turned in their neighbours to the police, and to the FBI.

My father was a milliner, a hat maker. Being a milliner was pretty tough because he worked in the summer over steam to shape the hats. It was terribly hot and he had to commute long distances. Then in the winter months, he'd get laid off from work and rely on odd jobs. He eventually died at 53 from an industrial related disease; he got cancer from the dyes he worked with. I remember his hands had welts all over them from the steam burns, that's how the dyes seeped in. His work-life was a long way away from that of a therapist.

What was it like growing up in such a community?

I remember it as a great place. It was certainly influential for me growing up in an environment in which people had a very strong commitment to social change. During the Rosenberg trial, a lot of the organising for the protests against their arrest took place in New Jersey. There were meetings in our house, and discussions all the time. I remember during those times my parents hiding communists in our house. It was pretty intense and I can recall my younger brother once saying to my mother 'Can't you just be an American and stop all this'! There were some complications. In the local high school the Jewish kids were beaten up all the time and so our parents had to pay extra money to enable us to commute to another high school. But all in all the biggest legacy of those times for me and my siblings was the strong link to commitments to social transformation.

How did you come to be working as a therapist?

Well the first steps involved working in the welfare department in New York City. During this job I became very involved in the union until I was actually fired whilst making a speech on a desk. Being fired actually terrified me. I was 22 years old and I'd lost my job. I had heard that once you were fired from a civil service job it was really hard to find more work. Fortunately, though I was reinstated when the dispute that I was speaking about was settled.

Around this time I decided to go to social work school and when I finished this began to work in Buffalo, New York, in adoptions and with hard-to-place kids. These were mainly handicapped kids or African-American children. It was a complicated time when a lot of white couples were adopting African- American children and many African-American people were saying that this shouldn't be happening. During this time I gave birth to my daughter, and shortly thereafter moved with my family back to New Jersey where I began working in schools. While doing so, a colleague suggested to me that I consider training in family therapy. This took me to the Ackerman Institute to train initially with one of Nate Ackerman's original colleagues. The next year I had Olga Silverstein as my teacher and through her I became intrigued with the field of family therapy. I started reading everything and felt very excited. My training was a real treat as well as challenging.

I quickly joined every therapeutic team that I could. I worked with Olga and with Peggy Papp, as well as with Gillian Walker, Peggy Penn and Lynn Hoffman. I was also becoming more interested in ideas of feminism and was a co-founder of the Gender and Violence Project at the Ackerman Institute. This was with Virginia Goldner, Peggy Penn and Gillian Walker. The team became really important in my life. We gave each other permission to share all our professional dilemmas and struggles and it meant that our experience of working together was very meaningful.

It seems that the ways in which the Ackerman has organised projects around particular issues has been very generative. How did the Incest Project begin?

I was interested in seeing how far the idea we developed in the violence project could extend when children were directly involved. However, in the early months of the incest project, I realised that many families had been traumatised by the response of the social justice agencies investigating the abuse. Responding to the need to mitigate this 'secondary trauma' led me to form a consortium of agencies in order to provide a continuum of care for the families.

One worker from each of these agencies would came into the Ackerman Institute every Friday night, we called it 'the Friday group', and we would see families together. There were twelve of us and we would always eat together and speak openly with each other about our experiences. I found this an exciting, engaging and engrossing process. We became very connected to each other and ploughed into the complexities of incest.

Can you say a little bit about these complexities?

There are all sorts of complex dilemmas that we have struggled with. For instance, how can we acknowledge that there is a 'victim' in situations of sexual abuse, and at the same time acknowledge that there is also a relationship between the 'victim' and the person who has offended, that also needs to be attended to? How do we recognise the power that one member of a family may have over the victimised member, while not diminishing the complexities and multiple meanings of the connections between family members? How can we find a way to both maintain a strong moral position and yet respect the ways in which people may wish to remain in relationships with one another?

We have found it very helpful to understand these issues from a both/and perspective. We have found it important to acknowledge multiple descriptions. In the therapy room this means creating space for multiple descriptions to be articulated. So, if a child describes how her uncle abused her, we create space for her to not only speak about the effects of this abuse, but also enable her to talk about the range of feelings she has toward her uncle, the good and the bad. We are interested in how we can enable people to be able to hold onto multiple descriptions of relationships. And by having a chance to acknowledge multiple descriptions, we have found that it becomes more possible for people to develop greater skills in discernment of risk, or danger, and to make appropriate decisions.

This might mean women partners stop saying, 'I hate him, he's a bastard', to instead say 'Well, yes, I do love this and this about him, and this is why, but I realise that this is dangerous'. Or children might begin to say, 'I really miss my daddy but I don't think I can see him'.

Can you say a bit more about why you think it's important for therapists to be open to engaging with these complexities of experience in relation to sexual abuse?

In a practical sense, sometimes therapists can inadvertently contribute to an atmosphere in which people who have been abused can speak only of their anger towards the person who has perpetrated the abuse. And yet, those who have experienced abuse often feel all sorts of complex and sometimes contradictory things about their relationship with the person who has offended. Western culture is quick to offer polarised choices when perhaps what is more crucial in situations of trauma in relationships is to allow people to explore the multiple stories and confusing dilemmas. In our work, we endeavour to invite complex relational descriptions. This can include honouring the non-offending mother's attachment to the person who offended, and building the offending person's capacity for empathy, all the while prioritising the safety of the child and encouraging the offending person to take responsibility for the effects of the abuse.

How have you created the context for these sorts of complex conversations?

We made a decision that we would see the children and their parents both separately and together. And once we have spoken with the children on their own, we then engage in very interesting conversations about what the children want to share with their parent(s) and how we will go about sharing this. These conversations have proven to be very significant. When the child starts talking about what s/he wants and doesn't want to share we take the opportunity to talk about what this means about particular relationships. We might ask why the child does not want to speak to her mother for instance and we hear about the child's fears: 'she'll be angry', 'she won't understand', 'she'll think that I shouldn't have felt those feelings'. And then we begin to explore, 'Well, what do you think your mommy would do if she understood that you were worried about telling her certain things? Do you think we could talk to your mommy about this?' We move away from whatever the content was and instead begin to address the relational constraints in terms of the child talking to her mother. And we do similarly in terms of the mother relating to the child. In this way there is a constant flow between relational issues and content as well as between family and individual sessions. They are always linked. These are some of the processes we have been developing.

To end, Marcia, do you have any particular reflections on the state of the family therapy field these days?

For me, perhaps the most interesting aspect of the field at the moment is the way in which broader concerns about politics, race and culture are now being translated into therapeutic ideas and work. This is happening more and more these days, particularly inspired in the US by therapists of colour and by the work happening in Australia and New Zealand. That's something I really appreciate and I guess that appreciation is related to the stories I was telling at the beginning of this conversation.

17

The narrative metaphor in family therapy

an interview with

Michael White

Michael White lives and works in Adelaide, South Australia and is known within the field of family therapy for his explorations of the narrative metaphor in therapy. These explorations have occurred in collaboration with David Epston of Auckland, New Zealand. This interview took place in Adelaide.

Perhaps I could begin by asking you about what you see as some of the key themes that make up what is known as family therapy?

Family therapy is a field that is constantly changing, and has a great history of engaging with new and diverse ideas and developing innovative practices. There are a number of broad themes that can probably be traced through many of the 'schools' or traditions of family therapy thought and practice. One of these is that family therapy since its very beginnings has been vitally interested in how life is shaped by family relations. This involves considering identity as something that is achieved in relationship with others rather than something that derives from human nature, whatever it is that human nature is construed to be. Over time, the definition of the family has been expanded to include families of origin, families of imposition, and families of choice. And there has been increasing attention given to explorations founded on the understanding that today's family is itself a specific historical and cultural phenomenon, regardless of form.

Another key theme involves the understanding of people's problems within terms of the wider contexts of life. Rather than locating problems within individuals, family therapists have sought to identify the links between the problems people experience and the wider contexts of life, including the family, and the many other institutions of society.

A third theme involves meeting with families and other networks/ communities of people to address the problems in their lives. There is considerable emphasis given to the re-negotiation of people's identities within the context of their interactions with each other. These are all traditions of inquiry within the field of family therapy which strongly resonate for me and that have influenced my thinking and practice.

Apart from these general themes, there have been various specific developments within the family therapy field that I see as of great importance. For instance, the conceptualisation of therapy as a process of questioning, which derives principally from the work of the Milan Group. I still remember the day I read their 1980 paper, which has since become a classic. It was like experiencing a change in the weather. I believe that this contribution to the field of family therapy has been very significant.

There are also specific traditions of the family therapy field that are generally accepted and that to some extent are distinguishing of the family therapy endeavour. For example, there is some degree of commitment to the sort of transparency that is witnessed in the sharing of ideas about practice through the showing of videos of therapeutic conversations and in a willingness on behalf of family therapists to undertake live interviews with families and to be available to comments and feedback from other therapists and students. This tradition of transparency has led not only to a context of openness, but also to challenge and creativity that I think has been very important.

You said earlier that you believe that the field of family therapy is constantly changing, can you give an example of these changes?

One change that comes immediately to mind is the outcome of the influence of feminism in family therapy. Feminism has been perhaps the most extraordinary social achievement of the last few decades, and I think its influence within family therapy has been enormous. I believe that it has contributed to a sea-change, many of the implications of which are still being worked out. I know that there has been a backlash to feminist ideas, but, despite this, the ripples are ever widening. Feminism has changed, and is continuing to change, so much of what we think and what we do.

Within the field of family therapy itself there have been many contributors to this development, including: Olga Silverstein, Betty Carter, Peggy Papp, Marianne Walters from the Women's Project at the Ackerman Institute, Rachel Hare-Mustin, Monica McGoldrick and many others. In Australia, feminism had a particularly profound effect on the shape of family therapy practice through the early to mid-1980s. The 1980s' initiation of the women only 'Women and Family Therapy Meetings' ahead of the annual Australian and New Zealand Family Therapy Conferences was a very significant milestone in this development. In concert with this development, women like Kerrie James and others effectively drew the attention of the Australian family therapy community to the politics and power relations of gender, and they continue to do so. More recently, in our part of the world, the work of The Family Centre of Wellington, New Zealand, has significantly changed the family therapy field's ideas about issues of culture and partnership with other peoples.

Could I ask you about the evolution of the narrative metaphor in your therapeutic work?

I first entertained the story metaphor in relation to therapeutic practice when I was exploring some of Gregory Bateson's ideas – particularly his ideas about 'restraints of redundancy'. By this he meant that we carry with us a network of presuppositions that determine which events of the world we respond to. He emphasised just how highly selective we are in terms of which experiences of events we give meaning to and take into our lives, and described how it is that this network of presuppositions informs this process. Bateson referred to this network as the 'restraints' of 'redundancy' and talked about how these restraints play a part in transforming events into descriptions – words, figures and pictures. He also described how these words, figures or pictures become a story through our efforts to explain them.

I was very engaged in explorations of Bateson's ideas in the early 1980s. In the later 1980s, I began to relate more significantly to the narrative metaphor. This was partly due to Cheryl White's encouragement of me to privilege this metaphor in my work, which in turn was informed by her engagement with feminist writings. This interest in the narrative metaphor was also something that came out of my collaboration with David Epston. These were exciting times. David and I would be constantly phoning each other across the Tasman Sea with things to share with each other about the families we were consulting with.

One of the things that drew our attention to the narrative or story metaphor was the way in which it enabled the dimensions of time and sequence to be elevated and attributed greater significance in our understandings and in our work. The narrative metaphor takes in what is often referred to as the temporal dimension. It encourages a focus on the ways in which the events of people's lives are routinely coded into time, on the ways in which events are read into unfolding accounts of life. In this way, the narrative metaphor is less static than the metaphor of redundancy that I had found very interesting in Gregory Bateson's work.

What were some of the possibilities that this story or narrative metaphor opened up in your therapeutic work?

When people consult therapists they tell stories. People don't come along and sit there and say 'depression'. Rather, they say, 'I've been feeling depressed lately and it's something that has been getting worse. If I think back over the last three or four years I can pinpoint some events which have contributed to this. Let me tell you about them …' People are pretty specific about how these events of their lives are linked to each other in sequence. They are also very specific about time. A couple might say: 'So, this brings us up to three months ago. Then we had another crisis in our relationship, and that was back in June or May. Actually it was early June. Now it is September and let us tell you where we are at now in our relationship.' The narrative metaphor encouraged me to pay more careful attention to this temporal dimension of people's lives, and to the part that this accounting of events played in their developing experience of the problems they were seeking consultation over.

The stories that people tell about their lives are also shaped by particular themes – themes of loss, themes of tragedy, and so on. These themes have a historical trajectory and are engaging of many of the figures of people's histories. People's orientations to what they discern to be the problems of their lives are significantly influenced by these themes. Observations of this sort that are informed by the narrative metaphor made it possible for me to think more broadly about the problems that families were bringing to therapy, and, in response to this, I entered into more significant explorations of the various elements of narrative. At this time I also began to think through how I might be more effective in engaging people in conversations that would identify and give meaning to some of the more neglected events of their lives, and that would take these events into alternative storylines that would open up gaps in their otherwise problem-saturated accounts of their lives.

Engaging with the narrative metaphor in the development of therapeutic practice invites us to think about how can we encourage people to do what they routinely do – to place the events of their lives into storylines – but in relation to some of the more neglected events of their lives. This opens possibilities for the further development of therapeutic practices that are more de-centring of the therapist and centring of the meaning-making skills of people who consult us. This has been one of the big attractions for me about the narrative metaphor.

Are there any other things that attracted you to the narrative metaphor?

I often think about how there are many parallels between effective therapeutic skills and skills of literary merit. Good writers have a way of actively engaging the lived experience and the imagination of the reader, and of inviting him/her into new territories of life. There is something about the structure of the text in well formed stories that is exercising of the reader. The plot line is· not fully spelt out, and the reader has to fill many gaps in this plot line to stay engaged with the text. In well formed texts, these gaps are not so large as to frustrate and exhaust the reader, and they are not so small as to bore the reader. Not only does the reading of these texts of literary merit exercise the reader, but stretches them as well.

There are other gaps as well that are set into a well formed text. Good writers encourage readers to reach their own conclusions about the motives of different characters in the story, and about their pre-dispositions, their intentions, their attributes and traits, and so on. This triggers presupposition, which engages the reader very dramatically with the text. As a therapist, I believe I have a somewhat similar task. Within therapeutic conversations I see it as my task to build a scaffolding, through my questions, that is exercising and stretching of the families that consult me, and that make it possible for them to step into some of the less explored territories of their life.

Can you perhaps offer an example of how this takes place in a therapeutic conversation, of the ways in which you scaffold therapeutic conversations?

I might be meeting with a family that is struggling with a problem which is considered to be chronic and intractable. Having explored some of the effects that this problem is having on the lives of the family members and on their relationships with each other, I invariably discover that family members have already initiated steps that might not have been predicted and that are outside of the problem-saturated territories of their lives. At this point I usually find myself thinking about the sorts of questions that might assist family members to attribute significance to these steps – that would create the conditions that would make it possible for family members to load these events with meaning. I'd ask questions like, 'Does this fit with what ADHD had planned for James' life? Or does it represent some other development?

What do you think James? Were you doing what ADHD was telling you to do, or was this something else? Let's look at what ADHD has been up to in your life, and see if what you did here fits with that.' When we discover that we can't fit this or that event into the dominant storyline, then family members can be encouraged to assign these events alternative meanings. Further questions can provide family members with assistance in this. I might say, 'If we were to give a name to these steps, if these steps are to do with another theme in your lives, one that is distinct from the theme associated with the problem, what would we call it? What possibilities does this other theme potentially bring to your lives and relationships? Where do you stand on this development? For example, how is this for you, and how do you feel about it?'

Invariably family members judge such steps to be positive developments, and I can then inquire as to why they would judge them so. This inquiry provides family members with an opportunity to speak about purposes that they have for their lives that they have rarely, if ever, given expression to before. In response to extended conversations about these purposes, family members often for the first time name what it is that is associated with these purposes – specific dreams, hopes, aspirations, longings, pledges, visions and so on. The questions that shape this inquiry all contribute to the development of possibilities for family members to load these steps with significance. Once done, I am then interested in hearing about how family members prepared the way for these steps: 'What were the foundations that made these steps possible? What was it that went before these steps, and that prepared the way for them? I guess this didn't come out of the blue, so would it be okay if we had a conversation about what prepared the way for it?' And so on. We might then continue to reflect on these steps and on what they speak to about the purposes, intentions, hopes, values, and personal qualities of family members.

The questions that I have described here are but a small sample of what I refer to as 'scaffolding' questions. The first time I came across this term was about ten years ago when David Epston was talking about construction metaphors in therapeutic practice. In more recent times though I have been interested in other origins of that term, and particularly in the work of writers who have been influenced by the thought of Vygotsky.

What are some of the things that you are currently really enjoying about your work?

I really love meeting with the families that come to consult me. Every family I meet with is different and comes up with unique ideas to address their problems, many of which I find that I could never have predicted, nor imagined. It is in the context of these meetings that I always find new challenges for me to rethink the work that

I am doing and to make changes to this. I find that I am always having to question what I think.

And I have always loved engaging with ideas, and with the history of ideas, which is a treat. This pursuit of ideas often takes me to reading outside of the field of therapy. Having a sense of engaging with ideas that take me beyond what I routinely think is good for me. There is always something else to discover.

Are there any aspects of the work that you find less enjoyable?

In Australia we have a cultural phenomenon known as the 'tall-poppy syndrome'. This commonly used colloquial term refers to the practice of 'cutting down to size' any poppy that grows taller than the average. The naming of this phenomenon is in recognition of the fact that elements of the Australian community can be quite tough on its own people who receive significant recognition. I would have to say that this has had its down side for me, and that at times I find it quite wearying. However, this has only been a very small part of my experience, and I have mostly found Australian family therapists to be wonderfully supportive in a personal and professional sense, regardless of their orientation and their position on the different developments in the field here.

In closing, are there any reflections you would like to make about the family therapy field more generally?

When I think of the family therapy field I think of the people who make it up. I have personally experienced so much generosity from many figures in this field. For example, I believe that many people would be familiar with the part that Karl Tomm played in opening up forums for me to share some of my work, particularly in North America in the 1980s. His encouragement, friendship and challenge when I was young and shy was, and always will be, very significant to me. As I say this I am also thinking about my personal connections with other family therapists in many different places. As I think of these personal friendships, I realise just how many people have opened their lives to me. What's more, this has not been contingent on agreement. These people have included me in their lives while maintaining room for difference of ideas. These connections of mutual respect and personal friendship and appreciation of difference are something that I am grateful for. I cherish all of the 'into the night' conversations and all of the fun that we have had with each other.

It has been my experience that the family therapy field is one in which can be found support for people to explore a range of ideas, and the implications of these ideas in regard to practice. It is not a closed shop. I have really appreciated this. There are particular schools within the field, and I acknowledge that all schools have the potential to run into some of the hazards of orthodoxy, but there is no orthodoxy in a general sense in the field of family therapy. This fact is, I think, something worthy of celebration.

18

Working with words

an interview with

Peggy Penn

Peggy Penn, Director of Clinical Training and Education at the Ackerman Institute for the Family from 1985 to 1992, now runs a project investigating the uses of language and writing in family therapy. She teaches throughout the USA and Europe. She has authored twenty-five articles and co-authored, 'Milan Family Therapy: Conversations in theory and practice'. She is married to Arthur Penn and they have two children and four grandchildren, all boys. Recently, Peggy has also written a book of poetry published September 2001, entitled 'So Close'. The following interview took place in New York City. Cheryl White and David Denborough were the interviewers.

Peggy, your work in relation to letters and writing in therapy has been influential in the field, and I also know that you are now writing a book of poetry. Can I ask you about the history of your relationship with the written word?

When I was a child, I had an incredible grandfather, and because of him I could read by the time I was three years old. I was in the library by the age of four carrying out books to read! I recall that as I got older I would submerge myself in Alice in Wonderland and Dickens. I would take home these books and read and read and read. It was a way to run away to another part of myself.

By the time I got to the fifth grade at school, I was much taller than all the boys and most of the girls, and I was described as more like a horse than a child. I remember my mother saying that my height should be measured in hands not in inches. Some of the adults in my life were pretty tough and in the outside world

I often felt totally inadequate, like a sort of monster walking around. But also in the fifth grade my love of books led me to become the class librarian. And this librarian image of myself was important to me. In the library I felt comfortable with who I was. What's more, as librarian I felt a responsibility to read every book so that I could help others who visited the library!

That's fantastic! Libraries and bookshops are extraordinary places in the world aren't they? I always feel surrounded by all those characters, stories and ideas. I know that your first career was in the world of theatre, do you think this was linked in some way to your early love of stories?

Yes, many years ago my first career was in the theatre. I became completely occupied with play-writing and acting and so words and language and performance were central to what I was doing. My partner, Arthur, is a director and our lives for quite some time revolved around different plays he was doing. When I had children this changed somewhat. There was no way that I could be on the road with a child. One person in the theatre was enough of a challenge! I was determined not to have our family broken up by the theatre and the movies, so I would just drag them along. We learned to play poker in airports and we travelled together wherever we went – to England, to Italy and throughout the US. That's how we kept the family together.

It was also through having children that I became fascinated with child development and human behaviour. At the same time I was really frightened of psychoanalysis. I underwent analysis as everyone I knew did at that time, but where psychoanalysis terrified me, child development seemed full of mystery and intrigue. So I studied child development in between Arthur's movies. When the kids were old enough I then went and took a degree in social work and that led me towards working as a therapist.

After a few internships I went almost immediately to the Ackerman Institute in New York to do further training in family therapy. At the same time I decided I would also study with Jay Haley in Washington, so each week I would spend time in both New York and Washington. It was a busy time. When my father got sick it got more complicated as I was then travelling from New York to Washington to Pittsburg to New York. Finally I settled down at Ackerman and I've been there now for twenty-five years. Early on Olga Silverstein was my supervisor and I quickly became very attached to her, and I still am! I would watch her and Peggy Papp work together and I was fascinated.

In looking back, how does your history in relation to words and books and the theatre influence your work as a therapist?

I think it contributes to an awareness of the power of certain words and phrases. I am reminded of a woman who came to see me. She was soon to be married but found herself absolutely depressed on the eve of what was supposed to be a happy occasion. Her father had died one year previously and she found herself missing her father in a very significant way. She said to me, 'I'm just weighted with sadness'. There was a poetry in her words, a melancholic poetry and we spoke of the significance of the words she had chosen and her evocative expressions. Over time she came to understand her sadness as a form of reverence for her father and what he had meant in her life. Having an ear for the ways in which words are put together, for their poetry, can in a way assist in being open to the narrative potential in people's lives. In this instance, the story of sadness unfolded into a story of reverence. The woman wrote a letter to her father which was read aloud on the day of her wedding. Unpacking the words that seem to hold the most narrative potential, exploring what else they might signify is an important part of my work.

Can you say a little about the ways in which you use writing in therapy?

Writing can be an act of discovery. How many times do you sit down to write a letter and what you end up writing is a complete surprise? Well, this is often the case for me and so I have become very interested in inviting people to write letters in therapy. I have found that the medium of the written word can sometimes work better than conversation. When people in intimate relationships first come to see me, sometimes they bring with them monological descriptions of the other person: 'they are a tyrant' or 'they can't be satisfied', and the conversation can become stuck in these descriptions. I am determined to try and find other descriptions and in the process we write. For instance, if both people have been very angry at each other for a long time, I might invite them to draft an angry letter to the other person. Then I might ask each person to think about what would be the most important idea in such a letter. This would lead to conversations about what would make it most likely for the other person to really understand the significance of this idea, based on their knowledge of the other person. Through this process we start to generate much more complex descriptions, and the letters that they write to each other begin to change. We gradually move away from monological descriptions and this makes other kinds of relationships possible.

I also often ask a person who is grieving a death to write a letter and then to read this letter aloud to a witness group. This is a three-part process. First, there is the process of writing the letter. Second, when the person reads out their letter they hear it and experience it differently. And third, the letter is witnessed by others. This three part process is often a very powerful experience. About a month after such a ritual I often ask what it would have been like for the person who had died to receive such a letter, and what this person might say. I call this the 'Return Letter Voice', and I ask questions like: If you were to write back to yourself in your father's voice (for example), what might he say? This has proved to be a significant process for people to go through.

We're now trying to do some research to look at the effect of writing in therapy and the effect of reading aloud this writing in therapy sessions. I don't see writing as an end in itself, but it is a very creative process and it can create space for new voices, new perspectives and as this takes place new narrative directions become possible. It's not that I use writing with all my clients, but I might say, 'Does it make sense to you to write this out? Or to make some notes?'. And then people are free to take up this option or to choose not to.

I recall one man I was working with who said, in response to me suggesting doing some writing: 'I can never write to my mother, she was terrible to me'. So I said, 'Well, do you have any questions left over about that relationship?' He said, 'Questions? They're burning a hole in my heart!' So I responded, 'Well, would you be able to just write down those burning questions?', and so of course he did, and wept bitterly. Writing can take many forms, he didn't have to write a letter, I was just trying to find a way in which writing may be useful to him because it seems so helpful to many people.

I know that you are also very interested in listening, what role do you see listening as having in relation to therapy and writing?

Learning how to listen and to pay attention to the complexity of people's stories seems absolutely crucial to me. One aspect of social constructionism that really appeals to me is the idea that language and conversation are constitutive. The recognition that as we speak we make up our lives is wonderful to me and how we listen becomes all the more important. I am interested in how we can listen in ways that enable people to feel a sense of moral worth. That seems an important consideration to me and I think it is in some way linked to listening through our own stories. Stories influence how we listen, how we read, what we pay attention to, how we speak and how we write. I think it's so important for us as therapists to be aware that our stories are living antenna, always responding to the presence of many voices both in told stories and in written ones.

Thanks Peggy. It's been a great pleasure to speak with you today. Perhaps your book of poetry will soon be read by other 5th Grade librarians ... That is a beautiful story!

19

Parallel worlds and considerations of power

an interview with

Elsa Jones

Elsa Jones is a systemic psychotherapist and clinical psychologist who works independently in Britain and elsewhere as a trainer, consultant, and therapist. She has published many articles and chapters, as well as books on working with survivors of childhood abuse, on developments in the Milan-systemic therapies, and on systemic couple therapy and depression. The following interview took place in Oxford, UK.

Can I ask, first of all, to hear about how you came to be connected with the Welsh language and culture which I know has been a significant influence on your working life?

I grew up in South Africa, speaking Afrikaans, English and South Sotho and learning that different peoples live in very different worlds. South Africa is a country in which cultural differences and injustices are vivid and obvious. That is not necessarily the case here in the UK. When I moved here many years ago, and then began working in Cardiff, Wales, it took me a long time to discover that there was more than one major culture in existence here. The Welsh culture was initially invisible to me as it is to many English speaking people. And yet this Welsh culture, with its own language, spirituality and beliefs, is actually extraordinarily present once you learn about it. I recall standing in a shop one day when I heard two people talking behind me in a language I had never heard in my life. I was just dumbstruck. I spoke quite a few languages at the time and suddenly realised I had never even heard the language of the country I was living in.

This took place during an intensive campaign by the Welsh Language Society who were determined that people ought to be able to be served in post offices, banks and shops in Welsh. One aspect of the campaign involved imaginative non-violent protests, and my growing awareness was due to one of these campaigns.

Having discovered this other language, I soon learned more of the Welsh beliefs, including the belief that rather than there being this life and then an afterlife, there is instead a parallel existence, an other world which exists alongside this one. This is a spiritual belief and there are places and times of the year and frames of mind in which it becomes possible to step from the one of these worlds to the other. The Welsh community is alive with all sorts of stories about these steppings across worlds. I found this belief a powerful one, as it paralleled for me, my experience of engaging with the Welsh world. It had always existed in parallel to the English worldview, it was just that I had not known of it, or of how to step across to it. I then began to learn the Welsh language and Celtic culture has become increasingly important to me. So too has the metaphor of parallel worlds. It seems to me that so often we live our lives in parallel worlds to one another, and this is very relevant to therapeutic work.

I know that one of the areas you have focused upon has been people's differences in experience in relation to gender and culture. It would be great to hear about how these considerations have influenced your work ...

I was a feminist long before I became a family therapist and was involved with a multi-racial group in setting up one of the first feminist conferences in South Africa in the early 1970s. I think there must have been about 200 women at that event who met to begin to talk about feminism in its very early stages. And so, I have a long history of feminist commitment. And yet in the therapeutic world for many years I accepted the dominant idea which described issues of gender as political and not belonging inside the therapy room. It took me quite a while to begin to reject that position. It was the work of American feminist family therapists such as the Women's Project, Rachel Hare-Mustin, and Virginia Goldner that made it possible for me to begin speaking about issues of gender within family therapy here in the UK.

With the support of several colleagues, Gill Gorell Barnes and I started networking which led to the first ever Gender/Power conference here in the UK. These conferences continued for some time. We were determined that different voices should be heard within them, and that new people should therefore organise them each time so that they remained vibrant. These conferences enabled me to bring together two disparate beliefs that I felt strongly about. One of these was my feminist position and the other was my commitment to systemic thinking. Up until that point it was very difficult to bring these together because within systemic thinking there was a determination not to talk about relations of power within the family system. There was a determination to view the family system as a kind of level playing-field. I had been realising the ways in which such a belief colludes with dominant gender relations.

I don't know what it is like in Australia, but here in the UK if someone starts to question particular ways of working people can get very cross. New ideas, for some reason, are often perceived as a great threat. To begin to speak about issues of gender brought cries of 'that's not systemic', but it felt very important to me and other women that we begin to do so. For me personally, I had witnessed South Africans risking everything to make changes to that country, and it felt the very least I could do to make some contribution in bringing considerations of gender and power into the field of family therapy here in the UK.

Although it was a bit hard for a while, it no longer feels like that. It feels now that considerations of relations of power are part of the mainstream of the field. And this has allowed us, together with the shift into what we all call postmodernism, to begin to be much more creative and self-critical about our work. We are now more conscious of thinking about the process by which our attention to one aspect of someone's experience may exclude another aspect.

Can you say a little about how these considerations of power have influenced your therapy?

I am a white woman, of a particular age, and a particular class. In South African terms, I believe my whiteness overrides class indicators, but in Britain, people are very subtly skilled at picking up class indicators. All of these factors may act as obstacles to clients who consult me in terms of their capacity to work with me. I believe it is vitally important that we are aware of this and all of the subtle and not so subtle ways in which relations of power influence our conversations in the therapy room.

There are many possible ways of trying to address these. One way, which I am interested in, is to find ways of being aware of, and then declaring my prejudices/values in therapy in a way that invites clients to declare some of their prejudices/values. Once we have done this then we can consider if and how we can work together. This is true in relation to cultural/religious differences and also in relation to gender.

Recently, in supervision groups, workers who consult me bring with them either their own cultural genogram, or a map of their dominant current ideas, which they feel are shaping their work practices. In this way, when we consult about a particular case, we can place what the worker says in terms of the historical and cultural context of the ideas that are organising their work at this time. These are the sorts of approaches that become possible when it is acknowledged that the position of the therapist is not neutral, and that relations of power influence our values and beliefs.

What does this make possible in terms of thinking about gender relations in your work?

Recently I've been consulting to a woman and a man who have been working with a group of men who have been violent to their female partners. I consult with these two workers together but also separately specifically to talk about gender. The woman worker speaks very articulately about what it means to her to sometimes be in a room in which there are 'twenty-two men, twenty-one of them who are known to hate women'! Her dilemma is that she needs to protect herself against the misogyny that is in the room and yet if she protects herself too much then she's no longer available for the work. For the male worker there are different struggles. What he struggles with constantly is how to be a man amongst those men. He speaks about the degree to which he needs to acknowledge his commonality with them so he can work with them, and the degree to which he wants to repudiate them and hold them at a distance, at which point he loses his skills and competencies. How we as workers relate to these issues of gender, how we respond, how we structure our workplaces in order to enable us to work effectively, all of these considerations come into play when we acknowledge how relations of gender are a central part of our work as therapists. These considerations are vitally interesting to me.

I know that you have recently been involved in research work around the issue of depression. Would you like to say something about this?

Basically, the research I have been involved in, which is funded by the Medical Research Council and run by Julian Leff from the Institute for Social & Community Psychiatry, has been comparing the effectiveness of different therapeutic approaches for individuals with serious depression. What has been exciting is that the outcomes have been very positive for systemic therapy, both in terms of long-term effectiveness, and also in terms of cost-analysis. I'm extremely excited about this because here in

Britain people working in the health services are under increasing pressure to prove the efficiency of our work. This, I believe, is good and fine, except that most of the methods designed to prove efficiency do not have any way of measuring the quality of therapy. All that is measured is the economic efficiency. So, what I am excited about in relation to this research is that it looks at both the quality, the long-term effects of the therapy for the people concerned, and the economics involved, and in all these spheres the results for systemic therapy were very positive.

Another important finding from the research supported what The Family Centre of Wellington, New Zealand, have been saying about their work. That is to say, that when we look in detail at the lives of those suffering from depression, an overwhelming number of them are living in a context of considerable external oppression. In this way, depression does not simply involve an individual lack, or difficulty, or failure, but instead occurs in a broader social context. We must, I believe, find ways of acknowledging this. 'Depression' has become such a medicalised term, and yet looking in the dictionary I found that one of the descriptions given for depression is 'the condition of being pressed down'. I believe that this phrase fits far better than many of the medicalised descriptions currently utilised by health professionals, as it evokes notions of power and powerlessness. If we understand depression in terms of its social context, perhaps this will enable different sorts of actions for healing. Perhaps it will mean that we will begin to look for ways in which individuals and their loved ones and communities might be able to re-empower themselves and reclaim their lives from situations of poverty, unemployment, racism and histories of abuse, that have contributed to the depression. Perhaps we will begin to see that as therapists we have roles to play in addressing depression that have implications well outside the therapy room.

Thanks Elsa, that seems an appropriate place to stop. It has been great to talk with you.

20

The influence of Milton Erickson

an interview with

Jeffrey Zeig

Jeffrey Zeig is the director and founder of the Milton Erickson Foundation and the key organiser of the Evolution of Psychotherapy conferences which are held once every five years in the US. The following interview took place in Oslo during the Family Therapy World Congress, in which Jeffrey Zeig was presenting on the topic 'Hypnotising family therapists: Using practical lessons from Ericksonian hypnosis in systemic therapy'.

Could you speak a little about the work that you are doing and the legacies of Milton Erickson to the field of family therapy?

I am the director and founder of the Milton Erickson Foundation. I met Erickson in 1973, when he had retired and was not so popular. Jay Haley's influential book 'Uncommon Therapy' had just been released and I had been studying hypnosis and reading about Erickson. I wrote and eventually got to visit Milton Erickson towards the end of 1973. For the next six-and-a-half years, before he died in 1980, I did everything I could to learn from him.

I organised the International Congress on Ericksonian Approaches to Hypnosis and Psychotherapy in honour of Erickson in 1980. It was to be one more opportunity for him to see his friends, but unfortunately he died nine months before the meeting. Gregory Bateson was to be the keynote speaker but he died four months before the meeting! Still, more than two thousand people attended making it the largest conference ever held on the topic of hypnosis. The Erickson Foundation has continued to hold these congresses on a regular basis. Then in 1985 we branched out to hold a meeting called 'The Evolution of Psychotherapy' which featured twenty-five luminaries whose work had shaped the field of contemporary psychotherapy in the latter half of the 20th century including: Murray Bowen, RD Laing, Virginia Satir, Bob Goulding, Rollo May, Carl Rogers and Bruno Bettleheim. These are just some of the influential Evolution Conference speakers who have since died. We hold the Evolution Conference every five years.

In this way, the Erickson Foundation acts as a kind of multidisciplinary organisation. In addition to the Evolution of Psychotherapy conferences we also organise multidisciplinary conferences on brief therapy where we bring together leaders in family therapy who do brief therapy alongside leaders in psychoanalysis who do brief therapy. This is very much in line with the Ericksonian tradition. Erickson really didn't aspire in any way to have a school named after him. He was just interested in human responsiveness and how to help people to be more effective in their lives. But out of Erickson there have spawned at least six different therapy approaches.

Can you say a little more about this?

I will start with a little history. Bateson had actually contacted Erickson through Margaret Mead. Margaret Mead had written to Erickson in about 1939. They were both thirty-seven at the time. She said, 'I have been referred to you by Abraham Maslow. I am studying trance in Bali and I know that you know something about hypnosis. Please send information.' Erickson wrote back a fourteen page letter followed by a seventeen page letter outlining what the then thirty-seven year old Erickson knew about hypnosis. They established a collaboration when she brought some of her trance films to Michigan and they became life-long friends. Then, during World War II, Erickson consulted with Bateson and Mead as they had established the Centre for Intercultural Studies to study the Japanese personality and the German personality. They fed information back to the US War Department. So, Bateson, Erickson and Mead were long-term collaborators.

The original Macy conferences, sponsored by Josiah Macy (the owner of Macy's department stores), began in the 1940s and it was from these interdisciplinary conferences that cybernetics was invented. Bateson brought Erickson to the first conference and from these events many further connections were made. Erickson consulted with the Bateson Project in Palo Alto. Jay Haley and John Weakland soon became interested in hypnosis and started travelling frequently to Phoenix in the 1950s to learn what Erickson was doing. In this way Erickson's influence permeated the Bateson project.

One of the streams that then was influenced by Erickson's approach is that of the Mental Research Institute (MRI) in Palo Alto which was founded by Don Jackson when the Bateson project disbanded. Early members of this team included Jay Haley, Jules Riskin, Virginia Satir and John Weakland. In 1967, Jackson, still very engaged with Erickson's ideas, established the Brief Therapy Project at MRI under the direction of Richard Fisch. The team included Arthur Bodin, Jay Haley, Paul Watzlawick and John Weakland.

Haley then went on to form his own school of strategic therapy. In 1973 he published his ground-breaking book 'Uncommon Therapy'. Its first sentence defined strategic therapy as being when the therapist has a goal in mind and works to reach that outcome. This school of strategic therapy was the second school that was highly influenced by the Ericksonian approach.

A third school of therapy influenced by Erickson was that of neuro-linguistic programming. Bandler and Grinder studied with Erickson in 1974 and 1975 and they started modelling Erickson using Chomsky's transformational grammar as an approach to understanding communication. They modelled Satir and a number of other experts in therapeutic communication.

A fourth school that utilised the work of Erickson is that developed by Ernest Rossi. Rossi studied with Erickson from 1972. He wrote and edited more books about Erickson than anyone else. Rossi explored the psycho-biology of mind/body connections and developed a school out of this work derived on a foundation built on his study with Erickson.

Yet another related school is that of the solution-focused approach. de Shazer studied with Weakland and some of the ideas that inform the solution-focused approach derive from Erickson. The self-relations approach of Stephen Gilligan has Ericksonian ideas at its base. Finally, there is a school of neo-Ericksonians – people like Steven Lankton and myself who studied with Erickson and have stayed more true to the use of hypnosis. We still keep alive the practice of hypnosis although in my own practice I probably only use hypnosis about 15% of the time.

As you can see, Erickson was very good at having intellectual heirs. A lot of people found him very interesting, studied him and then expropriated some his ideas to develop their own approaches.

How did Erickson's work relate to the development of working with whole families?

As far as family therapy is concerned, it seems that Erickson was doing therapy relating to whole families very early. For example, in 1963 there is a clear example of him conducting family therapy through correspondence. He wrote a letter to all the members of a particular family, in which he addressed each member, using some of his metaphoric approach. The letter clearly speaks to an understanding of systemic dynamics. I couldn't tell you exactly when Erickson really started seeing whole families in therapy. He certainly didn't consider himself to be a family therapist. He was critical of people who were rigid in their approach – just seeing families wasn't Erickson's approach. He would see people in various combinations. He would do whatever was needed to affect systemic change. He didn't try to think or write in terms of systemic theory although clearly his practice was that of someone who was aware of the effect of context and social systems.

What do you think were some of the things that resonated so much for others in the ways in which Erickson worked?

Erickson was a singular genius when it came to therapeutic communication. His command of observing and understanding human behaviour and how people operate and change was phenomenal. People from various fields recognised this. He collaborated with Aldous Huxley, for example. People recognised that he was an original and that the ideas he was espousing were quite different from mainstream psychological thought which at that time was dominated by psychoanalysis.

In his days other therapists felt they needed to understand a lot of content before they could do therapy. Erickson, however, was doing therapy without much knowledge of content, just by understanding and working with process. Therapists at the time were working hard to delve into people's psyches and understand psycho-dynamics to understand why people were the way that they were. Erickson was far more interested in demonstrating how people's lives could be different without necessarily exposing or understanding the underlying psycho-dynamics. These were radical ideas at the time. While other therapists were interested in making elaborate diagnoses before they proceeded, Erickson demonstrated that you could do therapy quickly without having a lot of information as long as you were steeped in certain principles of human understanding and certain principles of interaction, like utilisation. Utilisation was one of the pillars of Ericksonian practice.

Can you say a little bit more about this principle of Utilisation?

Let me give you an example. A couple came to Erickson saying that the problem is the wife's alcoholism. She has a pattern. She spends all weekend long gardening while drinking from a bottle of whiskey that she hides in the garden. Her alcoholism is so severe that the couple comes to therapy. The husband has counselled, cajoled, and criticised his wife to no avail. He's explained that drinking is bad for the relationship. He has explained that it is bad for her health. But she continues her 'little hobby' of gardening and drinking. As it turns out the wife also has a complaint. It seems that all weekend long the husband engages in his 'little hobby'. He reads, according to her, 'dusty old books, dusty old magazines and dusty old newspapers'. The wife has counselled, cajoled and criticised the husband and has explained that his little hobby is bad for his health and bad for the relationship. Erickson also discovers in the initial interview that the couple has a camping bus but they haven't used it in years. He also discovers in the initial interview that they have an aversion, a hatred for fishing.

So how are you going to proceed in that kind of case? Are you going to analyse the dynamics of the symmetric escalation in their relationships? Are you going to analyse the psycho-dynamics of passive aggressive behaviours? Are you going to categorise the relational pattern as hostile-dependent? And if you use those formulations how will that help the people to be different? If you are immersed in a theory of utilisation then the idea is that whatever exists in the social system, whatever exists in the therapeutic context, can be utilised to effect change. So, Erickson's first intervention was that he told the wife to go out and buy a bottle of whiskey.

Now she is no longer buying the whiskey voluntarily, she is doing it under Erickson's control. Erickson also said that she was to hide the whiskey. Well, she was already doing that, but he said she was to hide it in the home. Now this was a little different. Erickson would make a small change in the pattern of behaviour as he believed this can have a systemic effect. Then, he explained that when the husband came home he would have one hour to find the hidden bottle of whiskey. If he didn't find the hidden bottle of whiskey within one hour then she could drink with impunity – something she was already doing – in the home. This changes the context, but the changes are completely under Erickson's control. The couple have been playing a game, if you like, but Erickson has just put a little bit of spin on the game. He has changed some of the rules. He has put it under his control and moved the whiskey from outside to inside. The wife does this for a few days and is delighted. But after a few days somehow it is no longer fun to find a place that her husband wouldn't be able to track down a bottle of whiskey within one hour. So they come back to Erickson for more therapy.

Erickson takes them to task. He criticises, he counsels, he cajoles them. He says, 'You must go fishing'. They say, 'We don't like fishing, we told you'. They say no. Erickson says, 'You will go fishing'. They say 'Well why?' And he says that it is the only proper therapy: 'Husband, if you are in a little boat there is no place for dusty old magazines, dusty old newspapers, and dusty old books. Wife, if you are in the middle of a lake in a boat there is no place to hide whiskey. Go fishing.'

So what does the couple do? The couple does exactly what they know how to do. They rebel. They don't go fishing. They go camping and in the process of going camping they begin to renew their relationship. In the process of taking interest in their relationship they discover they can give up their old little hobbies and start new constructive hobbies.

The principle behind this kind of intervention which is amusing, is based on utilisation. If they are playing a game, utilise it. If they are criticising, counselling and cajoling and resisting, utilise that. Utilise the patterns that exist rather than analyse those patterns. As he did this, he also evoked other principles of Ericksonian therapy, like speaking the patient's language, and meeting the patient at the patient's frame of reference. It is a very positive approach because it presupposes that the patient has a resource in their own history for changing. They know how to change, they don't need to be instructed. This is not a psycho-educational approach, it's not about teaching people how to make 'I-statements' or how to use communication skills. Instead it assumes that the therapist is the context and that the family is the patient. And, if the therapist can establish a potent enough context then the resources that have been dormant in the system can come to the surface and can be accessed.

Erickson's therapy often involved people taking action didn't it?

Yes, patients come to therapy because they believe that they can't change and they can't cope. Most psychological problems are 'believed in imaginings'. So, Erickson believed that psychotherapy needs to help people experience their ability to cope, to experience their ability to change. That sort of experiential knowledge does not come simply through verbal intercourse. It comes from experiential learning. Erickson was strongly into making therapy an experience of change: through the use of hypnosis, tasks, stories, metaphors, allusions he involved patients in the experience of change. If you want to be happy in life there are no rules to read. It is not like you can learn an equation, and if you take these certain steps you will be happy in life. Being happy in life is a little bit like learning to ride a bicycle. It is a more visceral learning. It is something that you have to be. So Erickson made therapy a way of 'being'. And therefore, he used tasks and other dramatic methods to elicit change. It was a more evocative approach to therapy.

Can you speak about some of Erickson's other legacies?

Erickson had a wonderful sense of humour, but he also had personal knowledge of pain and hardship. He spent the last fifteen years of his life in a wheelchair suffering the after effects of polio. He had a strong belief that you can enjoy life in spite of, even because of, pain. You can enjoy life in spite of, even because of, its limitations. And so his brilliance at therapy was not just technique. It was his entire orientation to life. Life may be grim but therapy can really be fun. That seems a significant legacy to leave.

Can I ask you to reflect a little on the state of family therapy?

Family therapy has demonstrated that you can intervene on the social system and produce unique individual change. That is an important legacy. People like Whitaker would only see families. He wouldn't believe in seeing an individual in therapy and would think only in terms of systems – the larger the system the better! But there are not many people now who are solely family therapists in this way. Most people use family therapy now only when it is called for in their practice. So I don't think that family therapy should really be considered a discipline anymore. It is more a way of understanding. It is one of the lenses through which we can understand life.

Family therapy burst into the limelight in the '60s and '70s and there was a tremendous amount of generativity among people like Bowen, Satir, Minuchin, Haley, Watzlawick. Now in the US, this generativity has dulled somewhat, especially where managed care and protocol-driven approaches have made therapists more into technicians than artists. You are now expected to have a protocol for any given condition and apply that protocol. The face of therapy has changed a little bit into this protocol-driven, technical approach. It is almost a medicalised therapy. You see the condition and treat the condition as if you were seeing and treating pneumonia. If the treatment is not empirically based then the medical insurance companies may not cover it.

I guess this makes people like me a little bit of an anachronism. I am staunchly in the camp of believing that therapy is an art and not a science. It is an art in the manner that parenting is an art, or being a friend is an art. It is not something that can be quantified. I believe that good therapy is closer to poetry than it is to science. Experts in the field of therapy cannot agree on what is the essential unit of change. Is it behaviour, cognitions, affect, attitudes, beliefs, the body, systems etc? Imagine trying to have the science of physics without being able to believe that electrons or quarks are the essential unit. If you have a field where the experts can't agree what the essential unit is, then how can you pretend you are conducting a science? Because of the way that things need to be quantified for third party payers, many people seem to be moving therapy more in the direction of science. I won't be walking in that direction.

21

Reconnecting with family of origin work

an interview with

Ann Hartman

Ann Hartman is an eminent lecturer, author, teacher and clinician in the fields of family therapy and social work. Ann was the Dean of Smith College School for Social Work in Northampton, Massachusetts, and currently is Visiting Distinguished Professor at Fordham University Graduate School of Social Service. Her books include, 'Family-Centered Social Work Practice' and 'Reflections and Controversy: Essays on Social Work'. This interview took place in Boston, Massachusetts.

I know that for many years you have been very interested in family of origin work. How did you first become engaged with those ideas?

My link to the field of family therapy began when I was the executive director of a community mental health clinic on Long Island. Sanford Sherman, a close colleague of Nathan Ackerman, was on the board of our clinic and he came out to train the staff in family work in the early 1960s. My first exposure to Murray Bowen, who developed this particular approach, occurred when he was a workshop leader in a small family therapy conference held on Long Island in the mid-sixties. Subsequently, I heard him present at Ortho (the annual conference of the American Orthopsychiatric Association). I became very interested in the family of origin perspective and began to work with families and professionals utilizing these ideas. In 1974, I joined the faculty of the School of Social Work at the University of

Michigan and before long, a small group interested in family therapy founded Ann Arbor Center for the Family. Besides Joan Laird and myself, two other 'founders', Fernando Colon and Eric Berman, were also interested in family of origin work and it became a key aspect of the Center. Not only did we work with client families, individuals, and groups from this perspective, but the entire staff of the Center met monthly for a three hour meeting in which we did family of origin work together. Whenever there was an issue in the Center, such as a debate over money, we would talk about how money was handled in our families of origin, what messages and family stories we had received about money, and what implications this might have for the present. When one of the co-founders left the Center, we all explored how leaving and loss was dealt with in our own families. This was a central part of the culture of the workplace and I think it is one of the reasons that Ann Arbor Center for the Family is still going strong after over twenty-five years. By doing our family of origin work together, we came to see our own and each other's lives in a wider historical context and this made a substantial difference in our personal and professional lives and in how we were able to work together.

Although family of origin ideas and practices profoundly influenced me, I was never engaged with these exclusively. In the early years of family therapy we invited many leaders in the developing field to come to Ann Arbor, present to the professional community, and spend a day working with our staff. We also attended training workshops around the country and read everything available as the family therapy literature exploded.

There were aspects of Bowen's material that I was not interested in, especially his emphasis on differentiation. I felt this concept was too pathologising and also gender and culture bound. One of the ways in which he would describe an 'undifferentiated' person was as a person who had negotiated away his or her self in the relationship system. But that's what many women have always done! Women are socialised to negotiate away the self in relationships. In fact such relinquishment of self is necessary in the care of an infant. Are all women therefore pathological? Further, I discovered in working with Asian-Americans and African-Americans how truly foreign and even shocking to them was the notion that they should 'take an I position' with parents and other older family members! What I was excited about in relation to family of origin work was how it could engage with the family, help family members make reconnections, alter relationships with family members, and develop new kinds of relationships.

The genogram was an extremely useful tool in this work and became a standard part of work with families. That, together with the eco-map which I developed in the early 1970s, formed a very helpful picture of the family historically and in its ecological environment. Joan Laird and I helped to bring these ideas and practices into social work, particularly through our text, 'Family Centered Social Work Practice', which was widely used in social work programs in the US and abroad. I think there are many similarities between our version of family of origin work and the re-membering practices that Michael White has introduced to the field.

Would you like to say more about this?

Yes I would! I have always tried to make the links between Michael's work in relation to re-membering and family of origin work, although I know that others believe these ideas are completely different! I'm not saying there is a continuity of thought between these ways of working, or that Michael White was influenced by Bowen's work, but I do believe that there are strong connections.

But let me start with what I see as clear differences. Bowen's theories came out of a biomedical model that focused on notions of what was 'healthy' and what was 'not healthy' in relationships. His theory of differentiation is very much a part of the assessment of pathology. I abandoned this aspect of Bowen theory. What I love about Michael's work is that it is not pathologising. It does not derive from any interest in determining what is or is not 'healthy'.

The second clear difference between family of origin work and re-membering practices is that re-membering practices expand the notion of family. Re-membering doesn't just involve biological family, or even non-biological family. It involves any crucial relationship in a person's history. These people are included in one's 'life membership club', which is a metaphor I very much enjoy. All of this is very different from Bowen's emphasis on the biological family.

So, undoubtedly there are these differences. Where there are linkages, however, is in the practice, in inviting the retrieval of connections, the re-joining of relationships that have been cut off in some way, and in refashioning relationships that have been constraining or troublesome. It is similar in the effort to understand the meanings of those connections. Family of origin work is intimately connected with narrative work as many of the narratives which shape our lives are family narratives. These family narratives can be enabling and expanding, and they can be constraining and oppressive. To revisit those narratives of our family lives, and best of all to revisit those people who were so influential in the formation of our identities, can be very exciting work. It can be an extremely important part of re-storying our lives. Another very important similarity is found in the fact that in Michael's work and in our family of origin work, the therapist or consultant is 'decentered'. It is the client that does the work, and real life is the arena for change.

Can you share some particular stories?

When you have been working with families for over forty years you have a million stories! Perhaps I should start with my own.

My parents divorced when I was very young and by the time I was a teenager, I had almost no contact with my father. In my twenties I went into psychotherapy. By then, I had had no contact with my father for eight years. But it never came up that perhaps I should see my dad. It never came up, I suppose, because in the psychiatrist's understanding, I was going to work out issues about my father in my relationship with the therapist through the transference. I sat with this psychiatrist for a couple of years and all it achieved was to postpone my getting in touch with my father. I was almost forty before I finally reconnected with him. The first weekend I spent with him was so much more meaningful than all of the time I had spent in the psychiatrist's office. It gave me the opportunity to develop new narratives about my father, myself, and our relationship. I had been cut off for over fifteen years and to reconnect with him, to realise that I was so much like him, although I hadn't seen much of him since I was an infant, meant a lot to me. I felt reconnected to him and at the same time was able to get a better sense of him as a complex person. I was so glad I did this before he died. If I had not, I believe that I would have always been cut off from a part of myself. All those stories, all those narratives, would have had no resolution. I was finally able to reinstate my father in my life membership club!

But there are other stories too. I remember working with a woman who was an artist. Together we explored her family of origin experiences. Her mother was dead and her father was in Scotland, but as we worked she was able to develop some new stories about her life and refashion some family relationships, particularly with her father. Her father, a retired seventy-year-old working-class Scottish man, was very interested in the work his daughter was doing and on a visit to the States to see her, came with her for an appointment with me. I learned more about his story that day. He was born in Spain where his father was working. He lived in Spain until he was around six when his mother died. He and his brother were sent back to Scotland where they were raised by their grandmother. Upon his return to the UK from the United States, my client's father decided that he would do his own family work. He traveled to Spain, to the town where he was born. He located some places that had been a part of his life and, most importantly, found his mother's grave. In the process he also got reconnected with his brother, from whom he had been estranged for many years.

When you are inviting reconnections across generations I imagine that considerations of history are vital. During the evolution of the field of family therapy there have been a number of key generational challenges, if you like, such as the movement against the Vietnam War – which in some ways was a challenge from one generation to another – and the second wave of the feminist movement, which in many ways questioned traditional ideas of family. How have these generational challenges influenced ideas about family of origin work?

I think every generation has challenged the previous one. Perhaps it's the degree or the openness of the challenge that varies. I'm from the World War II generation and those times posed different questions. The 1950s, after the war, were very oppressive for many women. There was such a push to return to a romantic idea of what the family was supposed to be like. I agree that it is important for us to place families, our own and those of others, in their socio-political context. I encourage my students to do that. One of the exercises I do in my classes is to ask students to meet in threes, with one reflector and one interviewer, and to identify and explore in some detail an historical event that they felt had considerable significance in their family. It's amazing what comes up in these discussions as they become more sensitised to history and its ongoing influence in the lives of families.

As you know, Australians at present are engaged in many conversations about reconciliation between Indigenous and non-Indigenous Australia. This process is asking questions of us as non-Indigenous Australians in relation to our family histories and how they are related to historical and ongoing injustice. I know that some similar processes are happening in this country. I have just been reading the book 'Slaves in the family' in which, as a Euro-American, Ed Ball is trying to come to terms with the legacies of his family histories, which include slave owning. Do you see such explorations as relevant to the field of family therapy?

No question about it. Some people have taken real leadership in this. Elaine Pinderhughes, an African-American social worker and family therapist, for example, has presented and published on narratives from her family of origin dating to the days of slavery. In the process she doesn't simply recreate her own life narrative, but reveals a history of injustices. It is very moving to learn of the personal strengths in the face of such tragedy. These explorations of history, and of how our past is influencing the present, particularly in terms of race relations, seem vitally important. And I do believe that the traditions of family origin work have something to offer in this process.

I'd like to ask a different sort of question now. For many years you have been a key figure in the field of social work. Can you say a little bit about how this field has changed, particularly in relation to women's issues?

Social work has always been a woman's profession, and I'm glad you mentioned it because, although I've been involved in family therapy for years, it has been social work that has been my major professional home. When I began in social work almost all the bosses were men, all the Deans in the schools of social work were men, and most of the university faculty members were men, while virtually all of the line workers were women. That's all changed. The ceiling has been well and truly cracked.

It's funny, it took me a long time to come to feminism. Not because I thought a woman's place was in the home – it just never occurred to me that women were oppressed. I was raised by a single mother who worked full-time, and, as far as I could see, did everything she wanted to do. I didn't see women as helpless or passive or oppressed, I simply followed the path my mother had created. It was really Joan Laird who heightened my consciousness in relation to issues of gender. For me, it was the issue of sexual orientation that had been paramount most of my life. I was much more aware of being oppressed as a lesbian than as a woman. I grew up before Stonewall. In fact I was a middle-aged woman before Stonewall. The oppression that I grew up with was enormously hurtful and drove me underground in many ways, but I have come to better understand the linkages between the many oppressions that exist in our society.

When I look around me now, with the prospect of civil unions, with proud lesbian and gay characters on regular television series, sometimes I can't quite believe it. It's a very different world. I know we have a long way to go and I know young people are impatient. I don't blame them. But if you had told me when I was twenty-five what the United States would be like in terms of lesbian and gay issues in 2001, I would not have believed you.

The changes in relation to these issues are raising very interesting policy questions. These are questions that social workers and family therapists should be involved with, such as the proposals for civil unions. I happen to be very fond of this idea. In fact, I think both homosexual and heterosexual partners should have civil unions. If people wish to link union with religion, they may also wish to have their relationships sanctified in the church. Civil union is a beautiful idea. For one thing, it disconnects marriage from religion, the state from the church. For another, it has such a nice sound to it, evoking the idea of civility. Marriage has not had a very favorable history. In terms of the possibilities of creating different sorts of families in the future, I'm all for civil unions!

Thanks Ann. As always it has been a complete pleasure to speak with you.

22

Talking with children and families

an interview with

Alan Cooklin

Alan Cooklin lives in London and has been an influential figure in the British family therapy scene for many years. In 1977 Alan was the first Chair of the Association of Family Therapy and at various times has been the Director of the Marlborough Family Service, and the Institute of Family Therapy. He recently edited the book, 'Changing Organisations: Clinicians as agents of change', and currently works at the Family Project at University College Hospital and Camden and Islington Mental Health NHS Trust. This interview took place over breakfast at the home of Alan Cooklin and Gill Gorell Barnes. Cheryl White and David Denborough were present. David was the interviewer.

Can we start with talking about your work with the families of people with mental illness? How are family therapy ideas influencing work in this context?

Recently, the government here has produced a statement which says that mental health services have a responsibility to work with the families of people with mental illness and yet in reality very few services are taking up this challenge. The Family Project in which I work has been an exception. For a number of years now we've been trying to create ways of working with families in which one or more member has a major mental illness.

The work that I have found particularly rewarding relates to families in which the parents are struggling with mental illness. Who helps the children in these situations? Who helps a child find ways of understanding what's happening when their parent has delusions – especially when the parent invites the child to join with the delusions? In Britain, the truth is that nobody does. The mental health teams don't respond to such situations because they generally do not relate to children. The child and family mental health services don't respond because the children in these situations often don't have any mental health symptoms. And the children and families social services don't respond because their priority is child protection in situations of serious child abuse. So, in reality, nobody takes responsibility for this group of children and families. This is one area we are trying to address.

Given your long association with structural family therapy ideas, are these ideas influencing this current work that you are doing?

Throughout my years as a therapist I have been intensely interested in a number of different ways of working. At one stage, I fervently believed in psychoanalysis and thought that through this theory everything could be understood. And then I became a zealot for structural family therapy. These were the two theories that I really engaged with. I do, however, recall a time when a group of us also experimented with being died-in-the-wool Milan therapists. We set up a supervision process but discovered that even as we tried to ask circular questions and demonstrate neutrality, we were really just continuing our structural work in a different guise!

Looking back, I'm not quite sure where my work departed from the structural approach. There are still elements of the structural approach that I find are useful, and I maintain a considerable respect for Sal Minuchin and his work. Over time though I have become less interested in considering families in terms of hierarchies. This is partly because families have changed so much. Over time I came to believe that structural theory was no longer relating to the ways actual families were structuring themselves. The other area that I believed was not developed in structural work was in relation to children's thinking. We hadn't developed a way of thinking about children's thinking, the ways in which they talk about themselves, and the ways in which therapists can engage with them. This has become a particular interest of mine.

Can you say more about this?

Traditional forms of discussion between adults and children could often be defined as didactic. They are often a one way process in which the child is supposed to be acknowledging the adult's wisdom! With this being the broader context of adult-child relations, it can take some work on the therapist's part to demonstrate to children that 'compliance' of opinion is not required in therapy. In fact, it can require considerable effort on the part of the therapist to convey that they would welcome hearing different points of view from the child as a basis of their discussions. This has become one of my key interests. How do you convey to a child in the context of a family, and with the parents' permission, that you do not require compliance, and that in fact you want to engage with their opinions, views and values?

This seems particularly relevant in mental health settings. There, the alternative to didactic conversations seem to be situations where professionals talk to children in very tentative ways, sometimes with a sort of funny high-pitched voice, often making hints at what a child might feel about a particular circumstance. This type of conversation, in my experience, often contributes to children freezing up!

So what alternatives do you explore in your work with children?

One alternative to both didactic conversation, and these pseudo-therapeutic conversations that inquire only about feelings, is what I call dialectical conversation. I use the word dialectic rather than dialogue because it evokes more clearly a sense of contest or debate of meaning. In my conversations with children, I am interested in engaging with the child's thinking in a playfully argumentative manner so that we can establish a dialectical relationship. In this relationship, differences are juxtaposed as a valid subject for comment and conversation. Only in such a context are we then able to talk together in meaningful exchanges about the particular circumstances of the child's life. The goal is to help the child to think about their circumstances, and to enable thoughtful conversations about their circumstances, rather than to elicit feelings.

There are a number of ways in which I approach these dialectical conversations with children. Firstly, I try to avoid 'problem orientated' descriptions. Secondly, I try to presume nothing and to be 'behind' rather than 'ahead' of the child. Thirdly, I ask questions that are easier to answer than to not answer. And fourthly, I try to make no interpretation or presumptions about a child's experience. But perhaps the key element is to find ways of challenging the child's expectations of compliance to adults. One of the ways this can be done is to allow a language of good-humoured 'contest' (as distinct from combat). Playful and 'silly' talk, albeit with serious intent, I believe can enable the therapist and child to build a relationship in which it is clear that difference of opinion is not only allowed but desired.

How did you come to be exploring these ideas?

My thinking about this has largely been influenced by listening to the ways in which children communicate amongst themselves. The language of children in the playground is very often full of contest even if it isn't combative. I believe it is through debate and the contestation of meaning that relationships of mutual respect can be formed. One way that I can really demonstrate a respect for, and engagement with, a child's thinking is to create a context in which I can question the child's logic and, importantly, the child can question mine. This can only happen if, as a therapist, I am able to convince the child that he or she genuinely has permission to maintain a different point of view from me.

So, in having these sorts of conversations with children, what are you hoping to achieve?

There are really two principal goals. The first involves moving the child away from being seen as a source of the problem, or a source of shame. If the child can engage in a form of conversation which stimulates pride in the parents, that demonstrates his or her thoughtfulness and opinions, then I believe the parents may be much more likely to tolerate the dissonance between their expectations and the child's behaviour.

And the second goal is that the sort of conversation I develop with the child might go on to act as a model of tolerable debate that can occur within the family in the future. Mind you, when I use the word 'debate', I am conscious that there are some problems with it. The goal in this context is not to create a contest of any type within the family, but to achieve a medium in which the juxtaposition of contradictions can somehow become tolerable and even enjoyable.

It'd be great to hear some of your reflections on current challenges or dilemmas that you think the field of family therapy might be facing ...

To be honest, I've become less and less interested in what family therapists think, because over the years I believe we have become somewhat arrogant about ourselves. Family therapy at times positions itself in ways that presume it is somehow superior to other mental health professions and I think this can alienate our colleagues. In fact, I don't really think about the field of family therapy any longer. Instead I think about 'What is the relationship of all the professions concerned with children and adults in our society, and how are these impacting on people's lives?' That is the key question for me these days. Currently, many of my most enjoyable work experiences involve working on teams with other mental health professionals or paediatric staff rather than in collaboration with other family therapists.

I also have a concern that the thinking within the field of family therapy is in danger of turning into a cul-de-sac, especially in the realm of theory. The ways in which some practitioners are engaged with postmodernist thinking is moving the role of the therapist away from intervention and towards dialogues with those with whom they are working. This is something that needs a lot of thought. In some situations, therapists and other professionals have a responsibility to intervene – particularly in situations of abuse. I know of a number of situations in which therapists have not intervened in situations of abuse, or they have felt so preoccupied with their role as being to ask questions, that they didn't actually say what they thought when something needed to be said. This concerns me.

At the same time, there are a number of positive developments. Here in Britain, for example, there's been a real mushrooming of family therapy posts in health services. No longer are posts designated generally for social workers and psychologists, but increasingly there are specific family therapy positions. This means that the fundamental idea of family therapy – that there is an alternative to traditional psychology and psychodynamic thinking – is permeating the general professional field. This has to be a good thing!

And I am also very interested in how family therapy clinicians can be agents of change within organisations. Over the last ten years I have had the opportunity to act as an organisational consultant for a number of multinational companies and this has been a considerable challenge. How the ideas of the field of family therapy can contribute to change in organisational structures and relationships is an exciting question. It's one which I am looking forward to more clinicians engaging with!

Thanks Alan.

23

An intimate history
of family therapy

an interview with

Lynn Hoffman

Lynn Hoffman is an internationally known lecturer on family therapy and co-author of various key family therapy texts, including: 'Techniques of Family Therapy' (with Jay Haley), 'Foundations of Family Therapy', and 'Milan Systemic Family Therapy' (with Luigi Boscolo, Gianfranco Cecchin, and Peggy Penn). Lynn was kind enough to agree to conduct this interview via email.

Throughout the many different twists and turns of the family therapy endeavour, you have played a crucial role in articulating new ideas and perspectives. And I know that you have just completed a new book. Could I ask you to speak a bit about this new book and your hopes for it?

I hope that 'Family Therapy: An intimate history' will become a 'beginner's book', not in the textbook sense but because it tells, in a personal and immediate manner, what it was like to take part in such a compelling movement. Each chapter is built around a story. Occasionally I am central, but more often a person or family that influenced me is central. The larger narrative is how people in a developing field left one set of givens, and migrated to something new.

You have witnessed, and been a part of, a number of the key shifts in family therapy over time. Can you say something about this?

Yes. For one thing, we kept changing sensory modalities. I only became conscious of the ocular style of knowing when some of us went to an auditory one. Instead of perspective and view, I began to think about hearing and voice. The experience-distant tradition of modern science gave way to a kitchen table tradition of proximity and speech. In my mind, this was linked to re-valuing the experience of women, who only recently, and in relatively small numbers, have been included in the world of literacy. However, it gave men a chance to try on some new garments too.

Then I noticed that another modality was beckoning: that of feelings and bodily senses. The conventional view was that the individual, through her neurobiology, was the container of traits like empathy or anger. The new idea was to see that the manifestations of emotion were not bounded by the skull or body or heart. They were, in fact, an interpersonal language. I invented the word 'tempathy', for 'travelling empathy', because I saw this idea being used in the work of innovators like Tom Andersen and Michael White. Tom Andersen would show his response to a powerful story in his body language, whether behind the screen or in the presence of the family. Michael White, too, began to talk about the value of being 'moved', as in transported to a different place. For me, this marked a sea-change in the manner in which we worked.

I have heard you describe how the field of family therapy seems to have developed what you call a 'reflexivity gene' that leads it to constantly change and mutate. Can you say something about this?

I don't know why this field did not go in the direction of previous psychotherapies that got stuck by following single geniuses. We certainly had enough single geniuses for that to happen. I think one reason is that we fell in love with philosophers like Gregory Bateson, who started to use new ideas about systems to explain what was actually going on between people. For a while, some of us did get stuck in the concept of homeostasis, but by staying with the actual experience, we realised that what I called the 'timeless circle' model had to change to a 'rivers in time' model. And so we moved to successor philosophers like Ilya Prigogine, who brought in time, and Humberto Maturana, who laid the foundations for the idea that we construct 'the world out there'. The modernist notion of objective reality was now in question and changing, so our field kept changing too.

Reflexivity was also built in on the practice level. Watching interviews on videotape, we got used to reviewing family sessions in the hope of finding out what was going on. Of course we never thought of asking the families to give their opinions. It was Tom Andersen who introduced the novel format of the 'reflecting team', which asked families to listen to the therapists as they talked among themselves, and then comment back. At the time, this practice felt like breaking the law, but it became adopted so widely and so quickly that for many a reflecting position became a way of life.

One of these shifts has involved moving from a modern to a postmodern paradigm. What do you see as some of the most hopeful developments in this shift? What is this making possible in the field of family therapy?

In my book, I do my best to show where the many arms of the Shiva-like concept called postmodernism has come from. I use the term to signify the trunk to which all these arms attach, even though social construction theory comes out of American pragmatism, deconstructionism is the child of the French philosopher Jacques Derrida, and poststructuralism stems from a group of American literary critics who were influenced by the writings of Derrida and Michel Foucault.

This movement has helped us greatly by its challenge to conventional frameworks. The main characteristic of modernism in human studies has been the supposed presence of some kind of internal armature or structure. Michael White has grasped that the poststructuralist enterprise can be used to question the inner artefacts psychology is built on, but he also tries to replace its objectifying language with a more human one. For instance, he goes to anthropology to find a non-pejorative phrase like 'thick description', which counteracts the 'thin descriptions' of clinical nosology. Another of his anthropological terms is the 'definitional ceremony', an activity that creates new communal and transformative spaces. He has at times been perceived as an alien to family therapy, with his different language, but the way I see it, introducing words from another lexicon is already a pattern built into our field, and is part of the reflexivity gene I spoke of before.

I know that you have a considerable sense of excitement about developments in the thinking in the field of family therapy at this time. Can you say a little bit about this excitement and how it is similar and different from the excitement of the early days of family therapy.

In the beginning, people who became excited about family therapy acted as if they were on a mission. I certainly did. That missionary feeling has died down, but what is still exciting is that relational thinking has become a worldwide movement. Like burrs that travel on the fur of passing animals, systemic ideas have been taken to many countries and have evolved differently in each place. People in the UK,

Ireland, Italy, Norway, Sweden, Finland, Australia and Canada liked the social justice implications of the way systemic therapists thought and worked. This is why movements like feminism and multiculturalism still influence our field. We seem to have blazed some sort of 'Silk Road', and new inventions like those attached to narrative therapy or reflecting teams keep being disseminated along it, even as the road evolves.

Thanks Lynn, we so appreciate being able to include your perspective within this book.

24

Anthropology, archives, co-research and narrative therapy

an interview with

David Epston

David Epston is one of the co-founders of narrative therapy and is widely respected for his innovative and creative work. He has introduced to the field of family therapy a range of alternative approaches including the use of leagues, archives and co-research, all of which he discusses in this interview. David lives in Auckland, New Zealand, where this conversation took place.

To begin, can I ask about how you came to work as a therapist when your initial academic background was in anthropology?

I think the transition occurred in a number of stages. Having been brought up to believe that the university was the repository of the wisdom of all ages, when I was appointed in 1968 as a junior lecturer to the anthropology faculty of Victoria University of Wellington, I was an excited young man. I believed all my dreams, and those dreams that others had for me, had come true. And yet, disenchantment set in pretty quickly. I was dismayed to learn that a university setting curtailed my imagination rather than giving it free reign. Looking back, I don't think I can recall a more unhappy time in my life.

So instead, I decided to travel overseas and I was on my way to Europe via Asia, when I stumbled into a job in Aboriginal Welfare in Darwin as an anthropologist. In hindsight, I doubt I could have had a more chastening experience. My job was as an adjunct to a demographic project which had me 'counting' Aboriginal people.

In the late 1960s, the last whispers of genocidal policies and thinking were still in existence. I recall a policy mandated to have departmental employees no longer refer to elders as 'boys'. All that I witnessed and participated in made me determined to equip myself to make some contribution in relation to people's lives. This led me to Edinburgh University to undergo a Diploma of Community Development. While studying there I was hoping to return to third world communities in a somewhat more enlightened capacity than as a servant of Australian Government policy in the late 1960s.

It didn't really work out that way though. After finishing my studies in Edinburgh I travelled to Canada and lived in Vancouver for a time before returning to New Zealand and securing a job as a social worker in a hospital. After working there for less than a year, wondering what in fact I was doing and moreover why anyone should pay me for my befuddlement, I decided to return to Europe to do a social work degree in a radical social work program at the University of Warwick. I found myself becoming engaged with family therapy, which made me very unpopular with my Marxist colleagues! It was during this time though that I made connections with various family therapists who were to prove influential to me, including Olga Silverstein and Anita Morawetz.

So when you ask me how I moved from anthropology to my work as a therapist, I believe that I went through a series of transitions. I gradually moved from undertaking anthropology as an academic pursuit, to instead finding ways in which anthropological ways of thinking could underwrite my practice as a therapist. To this day I refresh myself by reading anthropological texts because I find some of the debates in anthropology to be vitally relevant to the therapeutic realm, especially questions about representation. It's not as if I believe that anthropology has answered these questions conclusively, but I believe some of the dilemmas faced by anthropologists are shared with those of us working in therapy.

Can you say more about these dilemmas or questions about representation and where they have led your own work as a therapist?

The primary problem in anthropology is the politics of representation. In most anthropological research, the source of the knowledge remains concealed. The knowledge of the subject of the research is appropriated and talked up in professional texts, in professional ways. From my early engagements with anthropology, concerns about representation have never let me go.

Much of my work as a narrative therapist has been linked to my concern to act against this appropriation of knowledge in the field of the health professions. In acknowledging the alternative knowledges about life that are often co-created in re-authoring conversations, it then becomes a question of how to remain faithful to the sources of this knowledge, and how to do justice to the representation of the sources of this knowledge. This has led to the formation of leagues (for instance the Anti-Anorexia and Bulimia League) through which the insider knowledges of those who consult therapists can be represented in ways that acknowledge the authors of this knowledge, documents the very means by which it came into being, and also makes this knowledge accessible to others.

In turn, this has led to thoughts about archives and the role of archivists. The idea of archiving has always fascinated me and in many ways I see myself as an archivist, a co-creator and anthologist of alternative knowledges.

What does this metaphor of being an archivist or an anthologist of alternative knowledges make possible for your work?

An archive is a place where public records are held, and that in itself implies a different form of knowledge from that ordinarily engaged with in the professions. It implies a form of knowledge with an ethic of openness. The history of the library is a radical innovation. In nineteenth century England it was the basis of the democratisation of knowledge. The politics of a library, in which the distribution of knowledge is a public service rather than a private privilege, has always been intriguing to me. The history of the public archive is one within which I locate the work that I do. So that's one thing that this metaphor makes possible. It locates my work in a tradition and a history which mentors me.

Secondly, the metaphor of an archivist positions me as a collector and a sorter and this acknowledges the role and responsibility of discretion. There's a great deal of discretion about what's admitted into an archive and there's a considerable authority in this. An archivist isn't involved in synthesis so much. There's always more to come, the doors of an archive are always open for additions. An archivist seeks to augment the archive rather than to delimit it. To me, these are helpful guides in shaping my role in this work.

In order to archive solution knowledges, or alternative knowledges, I imagine a considerable amount of work needs to be done first. Can you speak a bit about this process and what it entails?

I've always thought of myself as doing research, but on problems and the relationships that people have with those problems, rather than on the people themselves. The structuring of narrative questions and interviews allow me and others to co-research problems and the alternative knowledges that are developed to address them.

The concept of co-researching is of absolute significance to me in this work as it structures another way of knowing and being together. It enables a relationship that brings together each person's purpose. The purpose of the person who comes to consult with me is generally to co-research ways in which to change their relationship with the particular problem in their lives. My purpose in the work, as well as to be a co-researcher in this process, is to try to add to the archive of knowledge around this particular problem as this is something that I will take forward through my work with others. Many people who have shared these co-researching relationships have moved on once the concerns we were researching are no longer a burning matter for them, and this is fine. But as a co-researcher, as an archivist, you have the moral responsibility of holding onto these alternative knowledges and making them available to others in ways in which your contributors confirm.

There are other ways in which engaging in co-research shapes a particular ethic of this work which I believe are significant. For example, co-research is informed by a particular type of inquiry. It is shaped by an ethnographic imagination, which again is a term from anthropology. In my teaching, I find this ethnographic imagination to be one of the hardest things to impart and I really don't know why this is.

Can you say a bit about what you think distinguishes ethnographic imagination from other forms of enquiry?

I think what distinguishes ethnographic imagination is its morphology, the shape that it takes. I think it requires a considerable discipline and a considerable humility. When an anthropologist visits the traditional peoples of the Tiwi Islands, northwest of Darwin, if they wish to engage with the meanings and understandings of the Tiwi they will be required to question all their own assumptions of life. The Tiwi people's ways of thinking and understanding life are based on completely different assumptions to those of us from western cultures. In order to engage with the meanings and understandings of the Tiwi an anthropologist would be obliged to have what Joan Laird calls an 'informed not knowing'. I think this is relevant to therapists working with those who consult us. Within the field of therapy, for many years there was an implicit assumption that in order to help someone you must know a great deal about them. What's more, if you found yourself in a situation where you didn't know enough about a particular person then there was a further assumption that you ought not show this lack of knowledge. Approaching therapy with an ethnographic imagination is a different proposition. However, 'informed not knowing' is still knowing a lot. To be able to assist people to know their own knowledge is a considerable form of expertise. It requires a different sort of inquiry, one that involves setting to one side one's own assumptions, making no pretences that you can know another's experience and 'walk in their shoes', but rather entering into an inquiry based on ethnographic imagination, whereby you seek their versions of how they go about the living of their lives.

The other relevant consideration is that in the professions we have been trained to think in comprehensive ways, in grand ways. I admit that this can be an attractive form of figuring things out. But I like the particular, the precise, the minute. I believe that therapy involves an ethnography of the particular, and the only way you can engage in such an ethnography is by asking specific questions. A lot of people have been schooled out of these sorts of questions. Sometimes people see the use of specific questions as directive, or leading. But I have no problem with asking questions that guide people to discover the grounds of their knowing. I have no problem with questions that lead people where to look, and that bring whatever is out there into their field of vision. I never know what's going to be found, but I believe I have a responsibility as a co-researcher to utilise a rigorous ethnographic practice.

Respectful curiosity is one thing, and a good thing, but I like to see it used with a considerable expertise. I believe what makes this expertise possible is an ethnographic imagination and an ethnography of the particular.

You have always been someone who has brought ideas and concepts from diverse fields to bear on your work as a therapist. I'd like to ask you how you see the family therapy field now. Are there things that are happening that you are particularly interested in?

What I'm interested in are those points where the historical jurisdiction of this field – in other words 'the family' – is breached. I'm for any transgression of that historical jurisdiction. When family therapy as a field came into being it was radical for its time. It proposed an alternative to individual therapy which was then upheld as the only form of legitimate interaction between therapist and client. But now the concept of family, especially the idea of the nuclear family, is no longer generally accepted as the primary descriptor of everyday life.

People operate in all sorts of social formations, like communities, clubs, teams. One aspect of narrative therapy has been to engage with these alternative descriptors of life and identity. People's identities are shaped by so many different relationships. I think we should be considering many different forms of community, and many different ways of calling people together, or convening people. And as for me, I intend to experiment with new technologies and all they have to offer by way of virtual communities or communities of concern.

Our work is now located far beyond the boundaries of 'the family'. In fact, if family therapists renamed themselves as 'social practitioners' or something akin to that, I'd be very happy.

25

Family therapy in changing times

an interview with

Gill Gorell Barnes

Gill Gorell Barnes is a Senior Clinical Lecturer and Family Therapist at the Tavistock Clinic, London. She also acts as Consultant for Training at the Institute of Family Therapy in London, and is the author of the recent book, 'Family Therapy in Changing Times'. Gill has been, and continues to be, an influential figure in the UK family therapy scene. This interview took place over breakfast at the home of Gill Gorell Barnes and Alan Cooklin. Cheryl White and David Denborough were present. David was the interviewer.

Perhaps we could begin by tracing how you came to be involved in the field of family therapy ...

As I left college, I was not really sure what I wanted to do with the rest of my life. When I went to university I read English and was tremendously engaged with the question of what goes on inside people's imaginary worlds. Knowing that I didn't want to become a journalist, and turning away from the Arts, I decided to undergo a Masters degree at the London School of Economics. This was an interesting training in those days because it was a combination of politics, social theory, psychology, human development, and old fashioned monetary and global economics. I found this extremely interesting because it invited me to think about the social dimensions of the problems people face. Whereas reading English was about being engaged with people's imaginary worlds, the Masters degree gave me a perspective on the external world.

During this course I worked for two years in child care in Islington. They took six of us graduates, none of whom had done social work previously, and offered us training and supervision while we completed our duties. This was in the mid-1960s during a time of profound social change. The first waves of migrants from the Caribbean were settling in London and the housing problems were dire. There were hundreds of students from Nigeria taking full-time degrees and their children were in awful pre-school child minding conditions. The child care department at that time was centrally involved in working with children and their families. I was working in the area of adoption and fostering, but I also had to 'inspect' child minders, and handle a range of residential issues like sexual abuse. This was all very new to me and I was lucky to have a good supervisor. Sexual abuse had not been 'discovered' by professionals in 1967 and there was no framework for thinking or talking about it.

When I finished my Masters degree I knew what I wanted to do. I studied 'mental health' and was fortunate in getting both my placements at the Maudsley hospital here in London. I did an adult placement and a child placement, before going to work with Robin Skynner at Woodbury Down. As I'm sure you know, Robin was considered one of the pioneers of family therapy in this country.

What was it like working with Robin in these early days?

Working with Robin was a real eye-opener as far as family work went, although there were aspects that I found frustrating. It seemed to me that our approach was too full of words for the client group that we were seeing. One of my lifelong passions is analysing text, how people talk about their experiences and how we attend to the way they describe it. Robin Skynner came from a group analytic background where the medium is words and the client group more likely to be middle-class. I felt at the time that the kind of 'group analytic' pronouncements that used to get made 'around' families were very inappropriate. The therapist used to make various pronouncements such as, 'This member of the family is holding the depression on behalf of the others', or things like that. We'd have these struggling, over-burdened mothers trying to keep their kids' heads above water and they'd receive pronouncements like this that made no sense to them. The therapeutic work really didn't seem to fit with their experience. The group work we did in schools and in the clinic, which was more reality based, also made me want to use a different kind of language.

At that time I was married to Henry who was a merchant banker and did a lot of business travelling. When I took a trip with him to the United States, I decided to try and visit the Philadelphia Child Guidance Clinic. Salvador Minuchin's book, 'Families of the Slums' had just been published in the UK and I had very much enjoyed reading it. He seemed to be working with inner city families in the US going through similar life experiences and difficulties to those we were working with in London. So when I was in the US I just rang up the clinic and asked if I could come and sit behind the screen and watch them work. I didn't know anybody, but they said 'yes' and so I spent three days watching their work. Everyone was very nice to me. I watched training films by Jay Haley and Braulio Montalvo. I watched Sal Minuchin work. I thought this was just great! The ways in which they were working and the interventions they were making seemed to fit with what the families needed.

I came back to England very energised as I could see the sort of difference I wanted to be able to make. At about this time, John Byng-Hall and Rosemary Whiffen, at the Tavistock, started an advanced training in family therapy. They also brought trainers over from the US so we had working lives alongside Harry Aponte and Marianne Walters, as well as much Ackerman training. The big difference about training at the Tavistock was that they had introduced videotaping facilities and one-way screens. By this time, I'd done three or four years of 'working with families', but without any facilities to monitor and scrutinise my work. Video provided this tool and revolutionised family therapy training in the UK. A back-and-forth process of participating in interviews and then observing the interviews on tape and discussing them with the supervision team began, and this has continued through to the current use of reflecting teams. These were exciting times and the energy led to the formation of the Institute of Family Therapy here in London in the mid-1970s.

How did your interest in focusing on women's experience within families take shape?

I missed the first wave of feminism in the 1960s so this was really linked to some major events which occurred in my own life. While my children were still young, my husband died very unexpectedly of a heart attack. Finding myself heading up a one parent family, I was incredibly conscious of what a difference it made having financial resources to draw upon. From that time onwards I became committed to thinking about women's experiences in families, especially women in poverty. So often women have so few social, structural and financial supports in making a home for their kids, although this picture has changed for the next generation in relation to many of the new technologies that offer women equal work opportunities.

Starting to think about women's experiences was for me incredibly interesting, as I started to understand my whole life in different ways. I discovered a language existed to describe positions I had previously found myself in, but had never been able to articulate. Elsa Jones, one of my great friends, helped me a lot in this process, as did Gwyn Daniel and Charlotte Burke later on. We worked in supervision teams together and would encourage each others' thinking.

At the same time we began to realise that the families with whom we were working did not fit 'conventional' ideas about families. In discussing ongoing clinical work, I became impatient about the misfit between much 'theorising' and our own clinical experience. Families who were consulting us were either headed up by lone parents, or were step-families with completely different extended systems than those we were familiar with. We became aware that the ways in which these families functioned were tremendously different from the ways in which family theories were mainly described. So I set aside time to do some systematic thinking. For the next two years, I took all the step-families who were referred to the Institute of Family Therapy into my supervision team. At around the same time I met a man called Paul Thompson, an oral historian, and we decided to do some research together on step-families. It ended up taking us five years, but this research finally culminated in the book 'Growing up in Step-Families'. I grew up with a father and a step-father, and a number of step-sisters who I was kept completely separate from because of family politics. And now I am part of two step-families, the one my mother married into, and the large family created by my partnership with Alan (Cooklin), including nine step-children. So, it seems kind of appropriate to have played some part in thinking and writing about these issues.

The other issue that you have written about recently has been separation and divorce. Can you say a little about this?

In 1999 within the Tavistock family therapy team we decided that each member of the team would explore in some detail how they used systemic thinking to work with families in relation to particular stressful life events. One group focused on illness, another on refugees, and Emilia Dowling and I decided to focus on divorce and post-divorce changes in family patterns. I saw this as a way of continuing the step-family work. For six years, one day a week, we saw children and parents who were going through the process of divorce and family re-arrangement.

This area is of course one of some contention – especially around the questions: 'Is divorce distressing for kids?' and/or 'What aspects of divorce are distressing?' In our experience, a number of issues are often blanketed under the term 'divorce', including domestic violence and child abuse, and so we took a particular interest in these issues. As it turns out, in one third of the families we saw and studied, the children had witnessed 'hitting' between their father and mother. In trying to establish what elements of 'divorce' are distressing, it seems crucial to investigate what degree of violence has been witnessed and experienced by children, and also the ways in which acrimony and hostility are expressed. Our research indicates that although the divorce itself is in some ways distressing the children, what is much more significant are the issues of hostility or violence and the level of acrimony between the parents.

These various themes of your work all seem to be related to how family therapy can adapt to the changing nature of families. Can you say a little more about this?

For so long, our field, along with mainstream journalism, continued to depict families in very narrow ways. Even five years ago there was an ongoing farcical situation in which it seemed to still be assumed by government that a family meant one house, two parents and children. My own family structures have never fitted such a definition, and the reality is that families these days don't fit with the assumptions of the past. For example, economic independence for women has led to many more women with young children leaving their husbands or extruding them from home, because they feel they can cope better alone. I've now become an advocate for fathers. One of my journeys has involved setting off to describe family therapy in ways that will enable us to engage with a diversity of families.

What is hopeful to me is that representations of family have changed dramatically in the last five or so years. You see this within the field of journalism as well as within family therapy. Now there's much more open discussion and debate. And this is needed because the situations can be quite complex. Take for example our statistics in relation to lone parenting. Studies have shown that more than a third of families in some London boroughs are lone parent 'families'. That certainly seems very high, but when you investigate what it really means, you discover that the statistics define a lone parent as anyone who is 'not married'. So in reality, many of the people classified as lone parents actually are not parenting on their own. They have simply decided not to get married, and not to declare two household incomes to the social security system, or they prefer living on their own, but share the parenting of the children.

What do you think these changes to families mean for the field of family therapy?

I think family therapy needs to concern itself with these changing realities. New cohabitation and marriage patterns, divorce and re-partnering, lone parenting and gay and lesbian parenting are all leading to many new family forms. I think family therapists need to understand these changes and what they mean for people's lives, as part of their own repertoire of 'thinking family'.

The other significant way in which families are changing relates to world migration. From my first work in Islington with immigrant families who were headed by the mothers of those communities, I have been personally involved in this area. The cultural complexity of the society here in the UK is literally changing month by month and I think this poses a major challenge for professionals. We must find ways of relating appropriately to expectations of families who are trying to reconcile traditions from more than one culture. In the 1990s I organised two conferences about taking race, ethnicity and culture into account within family therapy. They were both events that convinced me that we need to do much more work and thinking around these issues, as does my current involvement with asylum issues at the Medical Foundation for Victims of Torture.

Thanks Gill. It's been a pleasure talking with you this morning.

26

The Fifth Province Approach:
A realm of imagination and hopefulness

an interview with

Imelda McCarthy

Imelda McCarthy, alongside her Irish compatriots Nollaig Byrne and
Philip Kearney, have developed the widely respected model of family
therapy which has come to be known as the Fifth Province Approach.
This interview with Imelda took place at a cafe in Oslo, Norway,
during the Family Therapy World Congress.

*Imelda, to begin, can you speak a little about the origins of the Fifth Province
Approach?*

In 1981, Nollaig Byrne, Philip Kearney and myself decided that we would set up
a team to work with families in conjunction with the first clinical training program
in family therapy in Ireland. Lynn Hoffman was in Europe at the time and she
persuaded us to set up a Milan-style, non-hierarchical team. Nollaig, Philip and
myself all came from very different theoretical perspectives but we set out to learn
the Milan approach together, and had a lot of fun in the process.

During the first year of our program we met a wonderful family whom we
called the Royal family. The issues this family was dealing with were difficult
and complex and at times we were very insecure about what we were doing. The
grandmother of the family had committed suicide and we were worried that another
family member could also do so. At the same time, one of our young colleagues who
was a student in the program was depressed. We left one family therapy session very
concerned that a woman in the family might commit suicide. About two days later,

it was our young colleague who killed herself. It turned out that she had committed suicide on the anniversary of the date when the grandmother in the family had died. We were devastated, so much so that the team split apart for about six months. We all went separate ways trying to deal with this tragedy. It was our first training program and we really had enormous support from our then boss, Sr. Jo Kennedy, who has since featured in much of our written work.

When Nollaig, Philip and I finally came back together it was as if we had a new resolve. Ironically, we weren't afraid anymore. We received a number of referrals from families whose children had disclosed sexual abuse and we began to see them. Our project was born out of the tragedy. It was the fire that lit our souls. I think it helped us to link with those families where abuse had occurred and, rather than see devastation, we began to look for the strengths – the strengths involved in the young girls telling their stories, and by and large their families (especially their mothers) being able to hear them.

We just hid away in our rooms seeing these families. We told no-one what we were doing, but Lynn Hoffman and Monica McGoldrick kept reaching out to us and introducing us to people, until gradually we began to present our work overseas. For a long time nobody in Ireland knew what we were doing. For years and years, we would be presenting papers in different parts of the world while remaining completely unknown in Ireland. It is, I think, quite common for people to have complex interactions in their own country while being well received elsewhere.

Was it within this work with abuse that the metaphor of the Fifth Province began to develop?

Very much so. Anyone who works with the disclosure of abuse knows that there is always an enormous number of professionals involved with these families, all with a different view as to what action should be taken. We very quickly found ourselves embroiled in various professional squabbles and realised that we had to do something to change this. Philip, who is fantastic at reading widely and bringing articles to our attention, found a book of Irish studies called, 'The Crane Bag', which was edited by two philosophers. Within this book was the story of the Fifth Province.

The Fifth Province of Ireland was thought to have existed in the centre of Ireland where the four provinces meet. There is actually a hill in the middle of Ireland at this spot called the hill of Uisneach, now the Hill of the Kings, and this is thought to be the sacred site of the Druids. The Fifth Province, according to the legend told by these philosophers, was a place where the Kings and Chieftains came to receive counsel and to talk out their conflicts. It was a place where no weapons were permitted. We have never more fully researched the origins of this story but we derive a great deal of meaning from it. The hill of Uisneach is certainly a sacred site. It is on a very high elevation from where you can see across many midland counties.

We liked the metaphor of the Fifth Province very much. As we were dealing with the multi-person systems and the widely opposing views, we started to imagine what it would be like if we could create a kind of safe holding place for everyone involved. We started to imagine what it might be like to create a place where multiple viewpoints could be considered, and where options were searched for that would reduce the chances of an escalation of conflict. We started to plan how we could create a therapeutic Fifth Province.

Could you say a little about the broader context of the work around abuse that you were doing at this time?

We knew that the conversations we were having around abuse were risky conversations. This was the early 1980s when the incidence of sexual abuse was only just beginning to become known in Ireland. Nobody really knew what to do. There was a lot of psychoanalytic literature about, but this didn't appeal to us. We were looking for new ideas.

The Ireland of the early 1980s was quite a difficult place to live. There was an economic recession and the national self confidence wasn't really high. The abuse of women and children was being talked about for the first time during the '70s and early '80s and we were losing a lot of our young people to emigration. There was a sense of terrible uncertainty in the country.

Turning to the cultural metaphor of the Fifth Province in this context was symbolic of seeking hope. We were seeking a province of imagination and possibility. We were seeking pathways towards a more pluralistic society. And we were searching for a province in which ethical choices would be made in terms of the inclusion of the other.

Can you talk a little about the approaches to therapy that developed once you stepped into the metaphor of the Fifth Province?

From our very early days we were fascinated with words and the language people used. The Irish have a very rich history of poetry and ambiguity and at the same time a reputation for not expressing ourselves well, for not being clear about what we mean. We became fascinated with the language being used by families who were coping with abuse disclosure. Very often we found that they used evasive language or told tall stories and we weren't quite sure what they were saying. We decided to reclaim the word ambivalence from the clutches of psychology and celebrate it as an Irish resource!

We were put off with a lot of things we were reading in journals about how the Irish don't tell the truth, that they are not self-revealing, that they didn't know how to express themselves appropriately and are given to telling fairy stories and the like. We wanted to reclaim Irish uses of language. We also wanted to acknowledge that when people come to therapy around issues of abuse they are frightened. Why would they speak directly?

So, within the therapy itself, when families were using ambiguous language we did not challenge it, but instead decided to take it and exaggerate it further. Such a way of conversing is an Irish trait or tendency. We Irish love to blow stories up and make them fantastic! We found in therapy that if we really followed the logic of the story that was being presented to us and exaggerated it, then it was like we could walk with the people out to the edge of meaning. Usually what we found was that people would then begin to make different choices, less extreme choices, or to question the logic by which they had been thinking. We were fascinated by this kind of process.

It seemed to us that this way of working was like a moving with people rather than a moving against people. When people saw the consequences of their belief systems they could then decide whether they wanted them or not. This was linked to a form of questioning we called 'questioning at the extremes'.

Can you say a little more about that?

Our way of drawing things out to their logical conclusion came to be called questioning at the extremes. For example, I recall one man who said to us that his wife would forgive him for anything. A typical question at the extreme in this situation might be: 'Would your wife forgive you if you made your daughter pregnant?' This sort of questioning involves moving with the line of the story to the logical extreme. We never ask these questions out of context. When we study our tapes we see that we only ask these questions when we have been given some sort of implicit permission. In the case above, the abuse was being denied at the time, and we felt free to ask the question.

This sort of questioning often seems to create a mental space or linguistic space for people to think differently or talk differently about situations. That's been our experience. These questions are not shocking to people as those in extreme situations have generally already thought of the worst scenarios. We need to be able to talk with them about the worst possibilities. Questioning at the extremes has often created space for new conversations.

You were speaking earlier about how this form of questioning also means issues can be raised without imposing meaning. Can you say a little more about this?

As a team we have talked a lot about the issue of imposition. The Irish history is one of nine hundred years of imposition and colonisation. We use the metaphor of colonisation to remind ourselves that everything we do in therapy is potentially colonising. Nothing we say or do is innocent. Our words have effects that we have to be responsible for.

As a team we value the idea of conversation being communion – something that people do together to make life worth living. For us, from the beginning, it has been very important to try to create an ethical space for these conversations. To do so we have focused on the politics of listening and the ethics of speaking. We can never listen from a neutral spot. We are all living within narratives that dominate our lives and that inform our thoughts. We need to be aware that we always listen from a position. The same is true in relation to speech. We ask ourselves, 'Are we speaking in a way that is inclusive of the other? Or are we speaking in a way that shuts the other off, or closes them down, or narrows opportunities for conversation?' This is always a challenge.

In our therapeutic conversations we attempt to work with all the different opposing viewpoints so that none are eliminated or belittled. We take care not to alienate anybody – whether they be the mother, the child, the father, the victim or the perpetrator of the abuse. We believe it is our role to create a space, a Fifth Province, where conversations that need to take place can occur.

This is not to say that we see all relationships as equitable. Adults are in different positions to children, men in different positions to women, people from dominant cultures are in different positions to those of minority cultures. We have never had an idea of equality. How things are spoken have different consequences depending upon who speaks it, how it is spoken and in what context. We have tried to always remain very attentive to the possibilities of us abusing power, as well the possibilities of others doing so.

Can I ask what you see as some of the current challenges that people are trying to address in family therapy?

I have a lot of thoughts about family therapy. In North America, the field appears to be losing energy and I feel there are a number of reasons for this. Firstly, I think systemic theory for a time became too narrowly defined, too rigid in relation to what constituted a system and a family. I think this meant a lot of people moved away from ideas of systems and mechanistic approaches.

Secondly, I think that family therapy is grappling with the changing conceptions of family. When you read family therapy books, even though they talk about multiculturalism, even though they talk about new family forms, the theory and practice consistently bring forward the concept of the nuclear family. We don't have good experiential models for bringing forth the kinds of families that people are living in during this day and age. I don't think family therapy has moved enough in the ways in which we talk and conceive of families. Of course this is not true for all family therapists but I think that is a contributing factor as to why family therapy in the US has lost energy.

There is also a dilemma I have with narrative therapy. I love the whole thrust of this way of working, but one of the things that I see occurring is that when students begin to externalise, it is possible for them to concentrate only on the larger societal discourses and miss some of the intricacies at the more local level. Problems are located as existing between the individual and the larger social situation or dominant narratives in society, and less emphasis is sometimes placed on the middle range of human networks that people live within. Whereas some other forms of family therapy have tended to blame families for the problems of family members, narrative therapy has not been at all interested in this. Perhaps, for some practitioners of narrative therapy, this has meant that they have missed out on considering the more immediate family. I'd be interested in your view on this ...

I doubt that I'm the best person to speak about that, but my guess is that it would vary enormously between practitioners. People have taken up narrative ways of working, like all other streams of family therapy, in a great diversity of ways. Some perhaps externalise in ways that risk missing the particularities of the person's experience, while others remain attuned to the language and emphasis placed by the person concerned, and explore the influence of the relationships that the person identifies as significant. I'm interested in your thoughts about how different spheres of family therapy have almost been grappling with opposite issues – on the one hand the family has sometimes been defined in narrow ways that have not fitted with the realities of people's lives, while on the other hand you feel that some developments in the field that have focused on the importance of considering the influence of the broader culture on people's lives may have moved people's attention away from family relations ...

I think it is a continuum. In Europe, I believe, the field is quite alive with all types of different possibilities. A great diversity of approaches are all popular – systemic therapy, narrative therapy and brief therapy. It is a healthy diversity. I would like very much to see practitioners from these different frames staying in touch with one another. I have really enjoyed that about this conference.

I also think that if we are serious about honouring ancestors in the cultural sense, as well as in relation to families, then we also need to honour the legacies of the family therapy field. There are some wonderfully rich traditions of practice and theory in the broad field of family therapy. There is also a lot of wonderful work occurring now that is spreading out into communities. The emphasis in the field seems to be moving beyond individual and family work into politics and communities and I think that is really hopeful.

27

Just Therapy

by

Warihi Campbell, Kiwi Tamasese & Charles Waldegrave (The Family Centre)

The Just Therapy Team, from The Family Centre, Wellington, New Zealand, consists of Warihi Campbell, Kiwi Tamasese, Flora Tuhaka and Charles Waldegrave. Their highly respected work, which involves a strong commitment to addressing issues of culture, gender and socio-economic disadvantage, has come to be known as Just Therapy.

The following piece has been adapted by Dulwich Centre Publications from a plenary session entitled, 'Cultural equity: The necessary step to cultural reconciliation' that The Family Centre gave at the Family Therapy World Congress in Oslo. This extract represents just a small fraction of the work that was presented. It is included here as it describes the history of the Just Therapy approach and therefore fits with the themes of this publication. It is the belief of The Family Centre that reconciliation and the ending of marginalisation will require members of dominant groups to take up their responsibilities to deconstruct their own dominance, and for these deconstructive projects to occur in consultation and partnership with people from marginalised groups. The presentation of The Family Centre's story at the Oslo conference was offered in the hope that it might offer ideas as to possibilities for other family therapists working on similar issues in their own contexts.

It was almost twenty years ago now, on one of our six monthly reflective retreats, when we realised that many families were approaching our agency seeking therapy for problems whose origins were external to the family itself. When we traced the origins of the problems these families were dealing with, time and time again we found that they were due to factors imposed by broader social structures. Families may have been presenting with psychotic problems, with psychosomatic problems, with behavioural problems, but when we traced the story of these ailments we found experiences of unemployment, of living in inadequate housing conditions, of being the victims of abuse, or of being a member of a culture that is marginalised by the dominant culture.

We consistently found that families who were coming to us for assistance with depression or ill-health were experiencing external problems such as poverty, ongoing racist experience, ongoing sexist experience, or ongoing heterosexist experience. It was these external factors that had made them vulnerable to depression which had then led to all sorts of problems of ill health.

We realised that the problems these families were bringing to us were not the symptoms of family dysfunction, but instead the symptoms of broader structural issues. We, like other family therapists however, were treating their symptomatic behaviour as though it were a family problem, and then sending them back into the structures that created their problems in the first place. We were unwittingly adjusting people to poverty or other forms of injustice by addressing their symptoms, without affecting broader social and structural change.

When we began to reflect upon this, we realised we were not alone. Much of the therapy that was being conducted with poor people or with marginalised groups around the world, was also simply adjusting people to problems caused by broader injustices. Twenty years ago, family therapists generally considered structural issues to be outside their domain, to be beyond them. In terms of therapy all that was seen to be dealt with were the immediate clinical issues. We had been no different.

We decided however that we were no longer comfortable with this aspect of our work and set out to make some changes. Critical amongst these were to make connections with the Maori community. We got very involved in the local marae (which is the gathering place for Maori people) and the local Maori community chose a worker for us. This was Warihi Campbell. They offered him to us and he became a part of us. We also began to make connections with the Pacific Island community and Kiwi Tamasese joined us. This began the process of altering the cultural combination of the staff so that it would more adequately represent the communities with which we were working.

The Maori and Pacific Island workers began to get involved in community development projects dealing with social issues such as employment, housing and anti-racism while we also continued working with families in therapy. Gradually, new forms of therapy began to evolve. Kiwi developed a Pacific therapy or Samoan therapy in relation to her own community. This therapy draws upon what is found to be helpful from western social sciences and rejects that which isn't helpful. At the same time it calls upon the knowledge of the Pacific Island elders and the traditions of Pacific people as methods of healing. Warihi did similarly in relation to ways of working in the Maori community.

Over a period of time we developed cultural sections: a Maori section, a Pacific section, and what we call a Pakeha section (a European or white section). Numbers of staff joined each section. Other Maori people came and joined the Maori section, other Pacific people came and joined the Pacific section. In this way we began to develop what we call cultural capacity.

We then faced new challenges and questions. How could we as workers, women and men and people of different cultures, protect against gender and culture bias in our work on a day-to-day basis? We recognised that even though all staff were committed to developed concepts of equality, unintentional impositions were still likely to occur because of our cultural histories. With sexist and racist assumptions an integral part of the society in which we were living, we knew that we were likely to perpetuate these assumptions in our life and work.

In response to these challenges, we developed partnerships and processes of accountability which we have written about in some detail. The Maori and Pacific Island sections are self-determining. The Pakeha section, because it is the dominant culture, runs its own affairs, but is accountable to the other two sections. Likewise, gender work including that carried out in men's groups is directly accountable to the women in the agency. This is to ensure that a therapy is judged as just, primarily by the group that has been treated unjustly. This is not an authoritarian process. We endeavour to seek a consensus that we can practice with integrity, and that satisfies those to whom we are accountable. The values of humility, sacredness, respect, justice and love, trust and co-operation are absolutely central to our processes of accountability. And our processes of accountability are central to our efforts in creating a just therapy.

Over a period of time, as we built stronger links with local communities and as we became active in the fields of community development, we decided that we needed to be able to make an impact upon policy makers. We found that it was possible through media coverage of community development projects to make an impact upon the public, but for a considerable time we were unable to influence policy makers. For this reason, we decided to become involved in social policy research. We found that if we could quantify problems then policy makers would understand. Policy makers are not usually moved by narratives, but they are moved by numbers! We became involved in social policy research and are now one of the leaders of the New Zealand poverty measurement project.

And so, in recognising that the problems families face are largely generated by broader social structures, The Family Centre came together to develop new forms of family therapy to work alongside community development work, social policy research and education.

Our change of focus also involved a change in language. We moved away from medical metaphors of cure, diagnosis and cases, and away from biological metaphors of systems and mechanisms. Instead, we developed a language that fitted our ways of working and articulated key values that underpin all of our work. These values or principles are those of Belonging, Sacredness and Liberation.

Belonging refers to people's sense of belonging – where they come from, who their people are, what their ancestry is. This is just as important for white people as anybody else. In family therapy, we believe it is crucial to understand issues of belonging. It is not that everything about our histories are good – often that is not the case. But we believe it is vital to assist people to find the liberative elements of their shared histories. In therapy, we seek to honour everybody's place and to ground people in a sense of belonging to their people, place and history.

Secondly, we have developed a concept of sacredness, in the sense of the sacredness of human life. People come to us full of pain and in vulnerability, as they do to other therapists. Their stories are given in vulnerability and in trust, and to us this is a sacred gift. We have found that in order to work together on issues of healing we have needed to develop a language of sacredness and ways to talk about spirituality. Initially, the Pakeha section saw spirituality as separated from physicality, as in the western tradition body is separated from soul. But for the Maori and Pacific members of staff, body and soul are fused together. It was unheard of to them for spirituality not to be a part of healing. In order to find ways forward, we have needed to develop inclusive understandings about spirituality, which we have described elsewhere. This process has certainly deepened the quality of our relationships and helped us to express together, in the workplace, the sort of relationships we are endeavouring to facilitate in therapy. By using sacredness and spirituality as our central image for an exchange within the therapeutic process we believe we are much more likely to treat people with a greater respect than if we applied the more commonly used mechanistic descriptions of casework.

The third principle which underpins our work is that of liberation. As therapists, we listen deeply to the stories that are told to us and, no matter how strange they may sound, we honour these stories and analyse the web of meaning that has created the problem. Then, in the best spirit of liberation, we facilitate new and transformative meanings that inspire hope and reconciliation. A metaphor of liberation evokes the choices people want, and the need that they have to be self-determining, either as individuals, as groups or as peoples. This principle of liberation also orientates us to our task of facilitating freedom from the problems which bring people to our door.

These are the principles upon which our therapy rests. They inform the questions we ask and the reflections we offer as a therapeutic team. These principles also inform the other work that we do – our community work and our social policy work. They guide us in our long term aim of transforming institutional structures so that they mainstream equity issues.

We need to be quite clear that we are not suggesting that what we do at The Family Centre is the only way, or the best way. It is just what we have done. It is one pathway. We have simply shared one story about the ways in which we have tried to find processes that enable reconciliation between cultures. We realise there are many different ways to grapple with these issues. But sometimes it is helpful to share a story.

Bringing it back home
to Australia

28

The Australian context

an interview with

Colin Riess

Australian history has certainly had a significant influence of family life - whether it's our convict histories, the dispossession of Indigenous families, or the waves of immigration that have subsequently taken place. Colin Riess is the Director of the Bouverie Centre, Melbourne, one of the first Australian family therapy centres and one that is still thriving. This interview, which took place at the Australian and New Zealand Family Therapy Conference in Canberra, focused on the question - how has the Australian context and social histories influenced the practice of family therapy in this country?

Perhaps we could start by considering some of the current issues that families who attend 'the Bouverie' are commonly dealing with, and then trace some of the social histories that may be contributing to the situations of these families?

I think one of the biggest issues to consider has to be that of ongoing socio-economic disadvantage, not only the physical effects of poverty but also the meanings generated by the experience of being economically marginalised. Families now struggle to survive and manage in a world that is increasingly dominated by a materialistic view of both people and things. I believe materialism represents a real threat to Australian families as it invites descriptions of children and adults more and more as either winners or losers. Increasingly, people are being defined in relation to their individual degree of success in acquiring material wealth rather than as human beings that belong to a meaning generating system (a grounded culture). For those who are economically disadvantaged this has real consequences. Another key current issue involves the fragmentation of families through the changing nature of work and employment. These broad social factors influence the kind of issues that families are presenting. They influence the degree of social isolation and lack of social support which many families are experiencing and which lead to specific health and well-being difficulties. Issues that come to mind that I believe are often exacerbated by our materialistic 'culture' include anorexia nervosa and depression, particularly for our youth.

Although we don't often talk about them, the broader culture's 'spiritual' or 'value' systems, through which people engender meaning in their lives, have significant effects on the problems that families bring to therapy. The individualism of Australian culture, for example, contributes enormously to the possibility of young people facing issues around their own sense of personal failure. Suicidal intentions and drug problems often reflect such a crisis.

Many of these broader issues can be traced to economic policies which have promoted the idea that the nuclear family ought to be a self-sufficient economic unit. Although this idea does not fit for so many Australians, it is a generalisation that has enormous effects on the commonly vulnerable groups of the community.

Having considered the social factors that may be influencing the sorts of issues Australian families are bringing to the Bouverie, is it possible to also consider some of the social histories that families are drawing upon to assist them in dealing with the problems in their lives?

I think every family brings its sense of identity with it to the therapy room, along with a sense of belonging to a culture and a sense of history. Often families are in some ways separated from aspects of their history and culture, but they always have their own set of values and things that are important to them. We generally see working-class families at the Bouverie and they commonly bring with them a sense of loyalty to family as well as to a particular Australian Rules Football club! Aussie Rules is a very important identifying tribal allegiance. Families from non-English speaking backgrounds tend to have more interest in religious affiliations and connection with their culture of origin. Sometimes this connection can be a source of good and a source of tension between generations.

Families also bring with them certain understandings of the helping professions - of psychiatry, medicine, social work and so forth. For some families there are histories which generate considerable and reasonable suspicion and uncertainty. This is especially true for families with negative histories of 'the welfare' interfering in their lives. And yet, other families will come along with a really optimistic and positive view about our capacity to be helpful. Some even have what we might consider to be an inflated expectation that we can somehow fix everything. Social histories have also played a part in influencing how families understand what we are doing together. This is something that we try to speak with families about.

Would you say that the Australian context, in all its diversity and variety, has influenced the practice of family therapy at the Bouverie?

It can be a little difficult to talk about these things in ways that do not appear glib, but I do believe that there are some general themes about Australian life that influence our ways of working. For instance, I believe that there is an egalitarian ethic in Australia, and a broad democratic ideal which means that, although there are structural differences between one's position as a therapist and the people one is working with, there is also a relative ease about professionals being open and reasonably direct, and an expectation from our clients that they can be direct and 'check us out'. Obviously this varies between different Australian sub-cultures. Some Australians may put professionals on pedestals, but generally speaking I would tend to say that Australian pedestals are not very high!

Australians also tend to have a healthy scepticism and an ability to make do, to tinker with things. There is an openness about shifting things around, checking things out. Therefore, when ideas have come from overseas we are happy to adjust, play and modify them without feeling like we are doing some great travesty to an artistic form.

Another significant influence is multiculturalism. Australia is now a profoundly multicultural country and the fact that therapists and families come from a diversity of backgrounds forces us to look at issues of culture. If you live in a mono-cultural world it is easier not to notice culture as an issue. Being confronted by multiple different cultures means that we have to constantly look at the assumptions that we bring to our work. I believe that this is a really helpful aspect about practising family therapy in Australia and particularly in Melbourne.

Of course, in Australia, feminism has also had a significant influence on the practice of family therapy. During the early development of family therapy, the theory and practice were pretty much gender blind. Early family therapy acknowledged the differences between men and women's roles but not the power differentials involved or the need for safety to be a starting point for therapeutic work. The influence of feminist family therapists changed all of this.

In the late 1980s there were many conversations about the need to consider safety issues when working with domestic violence and sexual abuse. Whereas early family therapy theory really disparaged the idea of meeting with individuals - there was a belief in only meeting with whole families - this changed for us due to the feminist analysis of domestic violence which articulated the need for separate spaces in order for women's safety to be prioritised and women's experience to be heard and acknowledged. This is just one obvious way in which feminism has directly influenced our therapeutic practices. We no longer hold to the traditional family therapy idea that we always need to be working with the whole family in the room - in fact in some circumstances this may be disadvantageous.

The influence of feminism also flowed over to considering other issues of oppression and how we as therapists can inadvertently marginalise our clients. It was the feminist movement that ushered in thoughts about other issues of power including issues of culture and sexuality.

I know that the Bouverie has worked considerably in relation to issues of HIV/AIDS. How has this work changed the practices of your therapy?

This has also been a significant influence. One of the challenges to family therapy practice posed by working with HIV/AIDS was a refiguring of the therapeutic relationship. We were seeing people over long periods of time and the therapeutic relationships often spanned such different aspects of people's life-cycle. Gay and lesbian people involved in the issue of HIV/AIDS are a very politicised group and were quite confident in making demands of health professionals to challenge traditional professional/client boundaries. We were soon understanding that it was part of our responsibility as family therapists to be attending funerals and visiting at the bedside. What's more, we soon couldn't imagine not doing this, and in this way our practices changed forever.

Have there been other ways in which those with whom the Bouverie has worked have changed your practices and thinking?

Certainly. Another area of our work has been in relation to mental health difficulties - especially issues of acute and chronic schizophrenia. The perspectives of carers and consumers have had a significant impact on our work, so much so that we have at times moved away from describing what we do as family therapy, to instead describe it as family sensitive practice. We learnt from families that traditional mental health professionals had been excluding the family members of people with serious mental illness through notions that only the family member with the illness was the client, and associated conventional notions of confidentiality. The challenges of the consumers and carers led us to revise notions of the therapeutic relationship towards more collaborative, informed and open practices. Their challenges were widespread and changed the ways in which we organised reception, as well as how we sent out flyers. We became more aware of our responsibilities to include the families of those who were experiencing serious mental health issues in every element of our practice.

In relation to sexual abuse work there have been different learnings. We have felt it was important for our service to maintain a capacity to work with all members of the family in relation to this issue. This often means different workers are working with different members of the family. We are committed to creating a bridge between those people who are working with the different parts of the family system. If or when a resolution occurs in relation to an acute issue, then it may be possible for there to be some contact between the adults and the children. By maintaining a bridge between the work happening with the different family members this enables the possibility of a useful, whole family process.

Lastly, we have a team working with the issue of acquired brain injury. In this area our workers are connected to families over the long haul. Situations may change over time and there is almost a spiritual dimension in terms of the loss and grief associated with head injuries. It is a life-changing experience for all the family members. The team has developed a way of looking at grief as a model for talking about acquired brain injury. There is a tendency in family therapy to need to feel as if one is continually contributing to change, whereas having grief as central to one's model brings more of a focus on acceptance. This has been another challenge for us.

We have certainly been influenced as much by those with whom we work as we have been by any other influence!

Thanks Colin. I really appreciate your thoughts about how the Australian context influences the practice of family therapy at the Bouverie, and I know you have to dash now to the next session!

29

Ways toward healing

an interview with

Colleen Brown

Colleen Brown is the founder of Killara Wangary Consultancy, which specialises in Aboriginal cultural awareness. She is also a well-respected and familiar figure within Australian Family Therapy. In 1997 Colleen received the Distinguished Service Award from the Australian and New Zealand Journal of Family Therapy for her contributions to the field. In this interview, which took place at the Australian and New Zealand Family Therapy Conference in Canberra, Colleen describes some of the experiences of Indigenous Australian families and her understandings of the potential of family therapy.

Understanding family relationships are a crucial aspect of family therapy. Could you speak a little about Aboriginal family structures and how these differ from the nuclear family models of the dominant culture?

The extended family is very significant to Aboriginal people. I am one of ten children myself. Both my parents were Aboriginal and I still look back and wonder how we as a family managed to remain intact.

I grew up in the days of the so-called 'Aboriginal Protection Board' which took Aboriginal children away from their families to be raised in Missions and in foster homes. I am thankful that we were left intact because we older children then learned to look after the younger ones. My elder sister and I each had a younger brother and sister to look after. They were more or less allocated to us. This was a really important learning experience, as when we grew up and had children of our own we automatically knew what to do with them. Whereas for those of our people who were separated from their families, who were put into institutions, they missed out greatly. They became just a number in an institution, rather than part of a family. They didn't have to look after anybody else, all they had to do was look after themselves. When it came to their time to get a partner and have children, many have struggled.

I have worked with many people who were stolen. I recall one young lass in particular who was one of 13 or 14 children who were all taken away. While she was in the institution she would dream of getting out and making a big home where all her brothers and sisters could come and live. But when she did get out she was lost and didn't know where to go. When I met her she was seven months pregnant as a result of rape. She already had one little boy. She wanted so much to raise the child but didn't know how to. She didn't know where to start. A few months later she had two children but could not cope. Eventually, she asked me to take care of her youngest child. I had to make sure that this was what she really wanted, but I was convinced when she told me that she was afraid of what she might do to him, what she might to herself, of what she might do to them both. Now her child is living with my son and daughter-in-law who lost their own child a couple of years prior. I said to the lass, 'Now your little bloke is in my family. I am Nan to him.' And she said 'Aunt, I couldn't have asked for a better family for him to go to'. She asked to go to the welfare to formally sign him over. 'I know where he is if ever I want to go and see him', she said. And I made sure that my son and daughter-in-law knew that the mother would always be able to see him. That worked out well. That's our way of taking care of children. If one family cannot cope, another one takes the child in.

When the children were taken by welfare it broke our extended families. The parents, grandparents, brothers and sisters were never allowed into the places where the children were put. They were kept at bay. A lot of our old people died broken-hearted because of what happened within the families. Now we are trying to find ways of re-building the extended families, re-making connections.

Is this in some way linked to your interest in family therapy?

My main aim with family therapy has been to be a teacher, to let people know about Aboriginal people and families without blaming them. If non-Aboriginal people want to learn about Aboriginal culture then they need to hear it from somebody who has lived it. I see myself as a teacher within family therapy and people have been very willing to listen.

One of the key things that I have tried to teach is how significant it can be for Aboriginal people to tell their life stories through art. There are many ways of finding healing. 'Therapy' does not just take place in counselling rooms. I have had many talks with people who have painted their way to healing, and I have presented on this process.

Telling your life story through art is a serious business. People have to think through where they are coming from in order to paint and when the picture is finished it can be shown to others. It can be healing of individuals and also offers a lot to all those who see the painting. Painting is both a healing process and an achievement. It seems to help people deal with the past and to paint a map for the future.

I'm a firm believer that there are many ways towards healing. Look at Archie Roach, the singer. If you listen hard to his words and his songs, they are all about his life. He has lived his songs. That's his therapy. Or look at Pauleen McLeod, the poet. She writes poetry about her life and this is her therapy. Therapy is about coming to terms with what we have lived. It's about finding ways for people to express the stories of their lives - through painting, through art, through music, poetry or through talking. I have been trying to draw people's attention to the fact that all these ways can be healing.

Not all of our people will feel comfortable in talking with a counsellor. We must find ways of keeping all the options open. For some, healing will be through writing. For others it will be talking or painting. I just encourage people to find their own way.

I know that you have done a lot of work around issues of grief. Would you like to talk about this?

As Aboriginal people we have had to deal with many types of grief. When Cook first landed in this country, the tribal people who roamed the land had their boundaries, but there were no fences. After Cook arrived the fences starting going up. Our people were kept off their lands. They could no longer eat what they used to eat, walk the lands they used to walk. The grieving began then. Then the assimilation policies took people from their homes and out of sight, out of mind, onto the missions.

I think of the old people when they were told that they would be punished for speaking their own language. I remember hearing my dad speak to his uncle in language one day. It was the first time I had ever heard it spoken. When I asked, all excited, what they were saying, my dad said 'You should not have been listening'. They were so frightened of what would happen if they were caught speaking their language. There is a great sadness for me that many of us have missed out on our language. I go into the big cities of Australia and hear Greek, Italian, Chinese and of course English being spoken. All these languages are being spoken in our land. I think to myself, why did they ever stop us speaking our own language?

There are a lot of people trying to retrieve these languages now, but many of our elders are gone. Many of the languages are lost forever. For some people, re-learning language is therapy, re-learning culture is healing.

In the last ten years, I've had to face many losses. We all have reasons for staying around. I firmly believe that one of the reasons I'm still alive is to contribute to healing, to listen to anyone, from any culture, who wants to talk, and to try to encourage others to learn about Aboriginal ways. There are many ways of healing, I'm just trying to play my part.

Contact details

and

Related reading

Contact details

Tom Andersen: Institute of Community Medicine, University of Tromsø, Breivika, N-9037, Tromsø, Norway.

Chris Beels: 865 West End Ave, #1C, New York NY 10025, USA.

Arnon Bentovim: The London Child & Family Consultation Service, 97 Harley St, London WIG 6HG, UK.

Insoo Kim Berg: PO Box 13736, Milwaukee WI 53213, USA. Phone: (1-414) 302 0650, Email: IKBerg1@aol.com

Colleen Brown: 5 King George Street, Erowal Bay NSW 2540, Australia.

John Byng-Hall: 24 Shirlock Road, London NW3 2HS, UK.

Warihi Campbell, Kiwi Tamasese & Charles Waldegrave:
The Family Centre, Anglican Social Services, PO Box 31050, Lower Hutt, Wellington, New Zealand.

Gianfranco Cecchin: Centro Milanese di Perapia della Famiglia, 19 Via Leopardi. 20123 Milano, Italy.

Alan Cooklin: 89 Southwood Lane, London N6 5TB, UK.

David Epston: The Family Therapy Centre, 1-3 Garnet Road, Westmere, Auckland, New Zealand.

Gill Gorell Barnes: 89 Southwood Lane, London N6 5TB, UK.

Kenneth V. Hardy: Ackerman Institute for the Family, 177 E. 77th Street, Box 12, New York NY 10021-1939, USA.

Ann Hartman: 15 Frost Lane, Hadley MA 01035, USA.

Lynn Hoffman: 31 Crabapple Lane, Northampton MA 10160, USA.

Kerrie James: Relationships Australia, 5 Sera Street, Lane Cove NSW 2066.

Elsa Jones: Oak Cottage, Great Oak Road, Crickhowell, Powys NP8 1SW, UK.

Joan Laird: 15 Frost Lane, Hadley MA 01035, USA.

Elspeth McAdam: 49 Elm Quay Court, Nine Elms Lane, London SW8 5DF,
                         UK. Phone: (44) 207 622 2732

Imelda McCarthy: University College, Belfield, Dublin 4, Ireland.

Monica McGoldrick: Multicultural Family Institute,
                         328 Denison St, Highland Park NJ 08904, USA.

Salvador Minuchin: 308 Commonwealth Avenue, Boston MA 02115, USA.

Margaret Newmark: 865 West End Ave, #1C, New York NY 10025, USA.
                         Email: mrbeels@post.harvard.edu

Peggy Papp: Ackerman Institute for the Family, 177 E. 77th Street,
                         Box 12, New York NY 10021-1939, USA.

Peggy Penn: Ackerman Institute for the Family, 177 E. 77th Street,
                         Box 12, New York NY 10021-1939, USA.

Colin Riess: The Bouverie Centre,
                         50 Flemington Street, Flemington VIC 3031, Australia.

Sallyann Roth: Family Institute of Cambridge,
                         51 Kondazian Street, Watertown MA 02472, USA.

Marcia Sheinberg: Ackerman Institute for the Family, 177 E. 77th Street,
                         Box 12, New York NY 10021-1939, USA.

Olga Silverstein: 460 East 79th Street, New York NY 10021, USA.

Karl Tomm: #300, 2204-2nd St SW, Calgary, Alberta,
                         Canada T2S3C2. Phone: (1-403) 802 1680

Michael White: Dulwich Centre, Hutt St PO Box 7192, Adelaide 5000,
                         South Australia.

Jeffrey Zeig: The Milton H. Erickson Foundation Inc.,
                         3606 North 24th Street, Phoenix, Arizona 85016, USA.

Related reading

Ackerman, N.W. 1966: *Treating the Troubled Family*. New York: Basic Books.

Andersen, T. (ed) 1990: *The Reflecting Team*. New York: W.W. Norton.

Anderson, H. & Goolishian, H. 1992: 'The client is the expert: A not knowing approach to therapy' (pp.25-39). In McNamee, S. & Gergen, K.J. (eds), *Therapy as Social Construction*. London: Sage Publications.

Anderson, H. 1997: *Conversation, Language, and Possibilities: A postmodern approach to therapy*. New York: Basic Books.

Ball, E. 1999: *Slaves in the Family*. New York: Random House.

Bateson, G. 1972: *Steps to an Ecology of Mind*. New York: Ballantine Books.

Beels, C. 2001: *A Different Story: The rise of narrative in psychotherapy*. Phoenix, Arixona: Zeig, Tucker & Theissen.

Becker, C., Chasin, L., Chasin, R., Herzig, M. & Roth, S. 1992: 'Fostering dialogue on abortion: A report from the Public Conversation Project.' *Conscience* (Fall).

Bentovim, A., Gorell-Barnes, G. & Cooklin, A. 1982: *Family Therapy: Complementary frameworks of theory and practice*. London: Academic Press.

Berg, I.K. 1993: *Family Based Services: A solution-focused approach*. New York: W.W. Norton.

Berg, I.K., De Jong, P. 1997: *Interviewing for Solutions*. New York: Brooks/Cole.

Boscolo, L., Cecchin, G., Hoffman, L. & Penn, P. 1987: *Milan Systemic Family Therapy: Conversations in theory and practice*. New York: Basic Books.

Bowen, M. 1978: *Family Therapy in Clinical Practice*. New York: Charles Aronson Press.

Bowlby, J. 1969: *Attachment and Loss, Vol 1*. London: Hogarth Press.

Browne, B. 1996: 'Imagine Chicago: Executive summary.' For more information telephone (1-312) 444 9113.

Cooperrider, D. & Whitney, D. 2000: *Collaborating for Change: Appreciative inquiry*. San Francisco: Berrett-Koehler.

Byng-Hall, J. 1995: *Rewriting Family Scripts: Improvisation and systems change*. New York: Guilford Press.

Carter, E. & McGoldrick, M. 1980: *The Family Life Cycle: A framework for family therapy.* Somerset, New Jersey: John Wiley & Sons.

Cecchin, G. 1987: 'Hypothesizing, circularity, and neutrality revisited: An invitation to curiosity.' *Family Process*, 26:405-413.

Cooklin, A. 1999: *Changing Organisations: Clinicians as agents of change.* London: H.Karnac Books Ltd.

de Shazer, S. 1982: *Patterns of Brief Therapy: An ecosystemic approach.* New York: Guilford Press.

Dowling, E. & Gorell Barnes, G. 1999: *Working with Children and Parents Through Separation and Divorce.* London: MacMillan.

Epston, D. 1998: *'Catching Up' with David Epston: A collection of narrative practice-based papers published between 1991 & 1996.* Adelaide: Dulwich Centre Publications.

Epston, D. & White, M. 1992: *Experience, Contradiction, Narrative & Imagination.* Adelaide: Dulwich Centre Publications.

Faderman, L., 1999: *To Believe in Women: What lesbians have done for America – A history.* Boston: Houghton Mifflin Company.

Foucault, M. 1973: *The Birth of the Clinic: An archaeology of medical perception.* London: Tavistock.

Geertz, C. 1973: *The Interpretation of Cultures.* New York: Basic Books.

Goldner, V. 1991: 'Sex, power and gender: A feminist analysis of the politics of passion.' *Journal of Feminist Family Therapy,* 3:63-83.

Gorell Barnes, G., Thompson, P., Daniel, G. & Burchardt, N. 1998: *Growing Up in Stepfamilies.* Oxford: Clarendon Press.

Gorell Barnes, G. 1998: *Family Therapy in Changing Times.* London: MacMillan.

Gorell Barnes, G. 2000: *Working with Children and Parents through Separation and Divorce.* London: MacMillan.

Goolishian, H. & Anderson, H. 1987: 'Language systems and therapy: An evolving idea.' *Journal of Psychotherapy*, 24:529-538.

Haley, J. & Hoffman, L. 1967: *Techniques of Family Therapy.* New York: Basic Books.

Haley, J. 1973: *Uncommon Therapy: The psychiatric techniques of Milton H. Erickson, M.D.* New York: W.W. Norton.

Haley, J. 1976: *Problem Solving Therapy.* San Francisco: Jossey Bass.

Hardy, K.V. 1995: 'The psychological residuals of slavery.' (video) New York: Guilford Publications Inc.

Hardy, K.V. & Laszloffy, T.A., 1995: 'Therapy with African Americans and the phenomenon of rage.' *In Session: Psychotherapy in Practice*, 1(4):57-70.

Hardy, K. V. & Laszloffy, T. A. 1998: 'The dynamics of a pro-racist ideology: Implications for family therapists.' In McGoldrick, M. (ed), *Re-Visioning Family Therapy*. New York: Guilford Press.

Hare-Mustin, R.T. 1978: 'A feminist approach to family therapy.' *Family Process*, 17:181-194.

Hare-Mustin, R.T. 1987: 'The problem of gender in family therapy theory.' *Family Process*, 26:15-27.

Hare-Mustin, R.T. & Marecek, J. 1990: *Making a Difference: Psychology and the construct of gender*. New Haven: Yale University Press.

Hartman, A. & Laird, J. 1983: *Family Centered Social Work Practice*. New York: Free Press.

Hartman , A. 1994: *Reflection and Controversy: Essays on social work*. Washington: NASW Press.

Hoffman, L. 1981: *Foundations of Family Therapy: A conceptual framework for systems change*. New York: Basic Books.

Hoffman, L. 1993: *Exchanging Voices: A collaborative approach to family therapy*. London: H.Karnac Books Ltd.

James, K. & McIntyre, D. 1983: 'The reproduction of families: The social role of family therapy?' *Journal of Marital Family Therapy*, 9:119-129.

James, K. & McIntyre, D. 1989: 'A momentary gleam of enlightenment: Towards a model of feminist family therapy.' *Journal of Feminist Family Therapy*, 3:3-24.

James, K. & Mackinnon, L. 1990: 'The "incestuous family" revisited: A critical analysis of family therapy myths.' *Journal of Marital and Family Therapy*, 16:71-88.

James, K., Sedden, B., Brown, J., Wearing, M. & Massam, M.: Yet to be published paper: 'Men's experience of their own domestic violence. Joint research project between Relationships Australia & School of Social Work UNSW.' Contact Relationships Australia (61-2) 9418 8800 for more information.

Jones, E. 1993: *Family Systems Therapy: Developments in the Milan-systemic therapies*. UK: Wiley

Jones, E. 1996: 'The gender of the therapist as contribution to the construction of meaning in therapy.' *Human Systems*, 7(4):237-245.

Jones, E. & Asen, E. 2000: *Systemic Couple Therapy and Depression*. London: Karnac.

Keeney, B.P. & Silverstein, O. 1986: *The Therapeutic Voice of Olga Silverstein*. New York: Guilford Press.

Laird, J. 1989: 'Women and stories: Restorying women's self-constructions.' In McGoldrick, M., Anderson, C. & Walsh, F. (eds), *Women in Families*. New York: W.W.Norton.

Laird, J. & Green, R-J. (eds) 1996: *Lesbians and Gays in Couples and Families: A handbook for therapists*. San Francisco: Jossey-Bass.

Laird, J. 1999: (ed), *Lesbians & Lesbian Families: Reflections on theory & practice*. New York: Columbia University Press.

Main, M. 1991: 'Metacognitive knowledge, metacognitive monitoring, and singular (coherent) vs. multiple (incoherent) models of attachment: Findings and directions for future research.' In Parkes, C., Stevenson-Hinde, M. & Marris, P. (eds), *Attachment Across the Life Cycle*, London, New York: Tavistock/Routledge.

Maturana, H. & Varela, F.J. 1980: *Autopoiesis and Cognition: The realization of the living*. Dordrecht, Holland: D. Reidel.

McAdam, E. 1998: 'The Appreciative Enquiry Project.' *Dulwich Centre Journal*, Nos.2&3:58-62.

McCarthy, I. & Byrne, N.O. 1988: 'Mis-taken love: Conversations on the problem of incest in an Irish context.' *Family Process*, 27:181-199.

McCarthy, I. & Byrne, N. 1995: 'A Spell in the Fifth Province.' In Friedman, S. (ed), *The New Language of Change*. New York: Guilford.

McGoldrick, M., Giordano, J. & Pearce, J. (eds), 1982: *Ethnicity and Family Therapy*. New York: Guilford Press.

McGoldrick, M. & Gerson, R. 1985: *Genograms in Family Assessment*. New York: W.W.Norton.

McGoldrick, M., Anderson, C.M. & Walsh, F. (eds), 1989: *Women in Families: A framework for family therapy*. New York: W.W.Norton.

McGoldrick, M. 1995: *You Can Go Home Again: Reconnecting with your family*. New York: W.W.Norton.

McGoldrick, M. (ed) 1998: *Revisioning Family Therapy: Race, class and gender in clinical practice*. New York: Guilford.

Minuchin, P., Colapinto, J. & Minuchin, S. 1998: *Working with Families of the Poor*. New York: Guilford.

Minuchin, S., Montalvo, B., Guerney, B.G., Rosman, B.L. & Schumer, F. 1967: *Families of the Slums: An exploration of their structure and treatment*. New York: Basic Books.

Minuchin, S. 1974: *Structural Family Therapy*. Boston: Harvard University Press.

Myerhoff, B. 1986: 'Life not death in Venice: its second life.' In Turner, V. & Bruner, E (eds), *The Anthropology of Experience*. Chicago: University of Illinois Press.

Newmark, M. 1991: 'A practical model for treating schizophrenia in the real world.' *Dulwich Centre Newsletter*, 4:29-34.

Newmark, M. & Beels, C. 1994: 'The misuse and use of science in family therapy.' *Family Process*, 33:3-17.

Palazzoli, M.S., Cecchin, G., Prata, G. & Boscolo, L. 1978: *Paradox and Counter Paradox: A new model in the therapy of the family in schizophrenic transaction*. New York: Jason Aronson.

Papadopoulos, R. & Byng-Hall, J. (eds) 1997: *Multiple Voices: Narrative in systemic family psychotherapy*. London: Duckworth.

Papp, P., Silverstein, O. & Center, E. 1973: 'Family sculpting in preventive work with well families.' *Family Process*, 12:197-212.

Papp, P. 1974: *The Process of Change*. New York: Guilford Press.

Papp, P. (ed) 1977: *Family Therapy: Full length case studies*. New York: Gardner Press.

Papp, P. (ed) 2000: *Couples on the Fault Line*. New York: Guildford Press.

Penn, P. 1982: 'Circular questioning.' *Family Process*, 21:267-280.

Penn, P. 1985: 'Feed-forward: Future questions, future maps.' *Family Process*, 24:299-310.

Penn, P. & Frankfurt, M. 1994: 'Creating a participant text: Writing, multiple voices, narrative multiplicity.' *Family Process*, 33:217-231.

Roth, S. 1985: 'Psychotherapy with lesbian couples: Individual issues, female socialization, and the social context.' *Journal of Marital and Family Therapy*, 11:273-286.

Roth, S., Chasin, L., Chasin, R., Becker, C. & Herzig, M. 1992: 'From debate to dialogue: A facilitating role for family therapists in the public forum.' *Dulwich Centre Newsletter*, 2:41-48.

Satir, V. 1964: *Conjoint Family Therapy*. Palo Alto: Science and Behavior Books.

Selvini-Palazzoli, M., Boscolo, L., Cecchin, G. & Prata, G. 1980: 'Hypothetisizing-circularity-neutrality. Three guidelines for the conductor of the session.' *Family Process*, 19:3-12.

Sheinberg, M. & Fraenkel, P. 2001: *The Relational Trauma of Incest: A family-based approach to treatment*. New York: Guilford Press.

Silverstein, O. & Rashbaum, B. 1994: *The Courage to Raise Good Men*. New York: Viking.

Tamasese, K. & Waldegrave, C. 1996: 'Cultural and gender accountability in the "Just Therapy" approach.' In McLean, C., Carey, M. & White, C.: *Men's Ways of Being*. Boulder: Westview Press.

Tomm, K. 1985: 'Circular interviewing: A multifaceted clinical tool' (pp.33-45). In Campbell, D. & Draper, R. (eds), *Applications of Systemic Family Therapy: The Milan method*. New York: Grune & Stratto.

Tomm, K. 1988: 'Interventive interviewing: Part III. Intending to ask lineal, circular, strategic, or reflexive questions?' *Family Process*, 27:1-1

Waldegrave, C. 1990: 'Just Therapy.' *Dulwich Centre Newsletter*, 1:6-46.

Walsh, F. & McGoldrick, M. (ed) 1991: *Living Beyond Loss*. New York: W.W.Norton.

Walters, M., Carter, B., Papp, P. & Silverstein, O. 1988: *The Invisible Web: Gender patterns in family relationships*. New York: Guilford Press.

White, M. 1991: 'Deconstruction and therapy.' *Dulwich Centre Newsletter*, 3:21-40.

White, M. & Epston, D. 1989: *Literate Means to Therapeutic Ends*, Adelaide: Dulwich Centre Publications. Republished as White M. & Epston, D. 1990: *Narrative Means to Therapeutic Ends*. New York: W.W.Norton.

White, M. 1995: *Re-authoring Lives: Interviews and essays.* Adelaide: Dulwich Centre Publications.

White, M. 1997: *Narratives of Therapists' Lives.* Adelaide: Dulwich Centre Publications.

Zeig, J.K. (ed) 1982: *Ericksonian Approaches to Hypnosis and Hypnotherapy.* New York: Brunner/Mazel.